Racism, Diversity and Education

Studies in Teaching and Learning
General Editor
Denis Lawton, B.A., Ph.D.
Professor of Education and Director
University of London Institute of Education

In the series:

Racism, Diversity and Education

Edited by
Jagdish Gundara, Crispin Jones
and Keith Kimberley

HODDER AND STOUGHTON

LONDON SYDNEY AUCKLAND TORONTO

Racism, diversity and education.—(Studies
in teaching and learning)
1. Minorities—Education—Great Britain
I. Gundara, Jagdish   II. Jones, Crispin
III. Kimberley, Keith   IV. Series
370.11'5   LC3736.G6

ISBN 0 340 34192 0

First published 1986

Printed and bound in Great Britain for
Hodder and Stoughton Educational,
a division of Hodder and Stoughton Ltd,
Mill Road, Dunton Green, Sevenoaks, Kent,
by Page Bros (Norwich) Ltd

Phototypeset by Macmillan India Ltd, Bangalore 25.

Contents

Studies in Teaching and Learning

The purpose of this series of short books on education is to make available readable, up-to-date views on educational issues and controversies. Its aim will be to provide teachers and students (and perhaps parents and governors) with a series of books which will introduce those educational topics which any intelligent and professional educationist ought to be familiar with. One of the criticisms levelled against 'teacher-education' is that there is so little agreement about what ground should be covered in courses at various levels; one assumption behind this series of texts is that there is a common core of knowledge and skills that all teachers need to be aware of, and the series is designed to map out this territory.

Although the major intention of the series is to provide general coverage, each volume will consist of more than a review of the relevant literature; the individual authors will be encouraged to give their own personal interpretation of the field and the way it is developing.

The Contributors

Godfrey Brandt — Lecturer, Centre for Multicultural Education, University of London Institute of Education

Celia Burgess — Member of project team, ILEA Primary Curriculum Development Project

Peter Fraser — Research Officer attached to Centre for Multicultural Education, University of London Institute of Education

Jagdish Gundara — Head of Centre for Multicultural Education, University of London Institute of Education

Crispin Jones — Lecturer, Department of International and Comparative Education, University of London Institute of Education

Keith Kimberley — Lecturer, Department of English and Media Studies, University of London Institute of Education

Gillian Klein — Librarian, ILEA Learning Resources Branch

Terry Mears — Secondary science teacher, Bristol, Avon Education Authority

Eigil Pedersen — Professor of Education, McGill University, Montreal, Quebec, Canada

Tom Vassen — Deputy Headteacher, Haselrigge Junior School, ILEA

Abbreviations

ACER	Afro-Caribbean Educational Resource project
ALTARF	All London Teachers against Racism and Fascism
APU	Assessment of Performance Unit
BEC	*See* BTEC
BTEC	Business and Technician Education Council
CARF	Campaign against Racism and Fascism
CCCS	Centre for Contemporary Cultural Studies
CGLI	City and Guilds of London Institute
CPVE	Certificate of Pre-vocational Education
CSE	Certificate of Secondary Education
CTA	Caribbean Teachers Association
DES	Department of Education and Science
DoE	Department of Employment
ESL	English as a Second Language
ESN	Educationally subnormal
FE and T	Further Education and Training
FEU	Further Education Unit
GCE	General Certificate of Education
ILEA	Inner London Education Authority
LEA	Local Education Authority
MSC	Manpower Services Commission
NAME	National Anti-racist Movement in Education
NFER	National Foundation for Educational Research
OWAAD	Organisation of Women of Asian and African Descent
PEP	Political and Economic Planning Unit
TEC	*See* BTEC
TSD	Training Services Department
TVEI	Technical and Vocational Education Initiative
UVP	Unified Vocational Preparation
WEEP	Work Experience on Employers' Premises
YOP	Youth Opportunities Programme
YTS	Youth Training Scheme

Introduction

The last decade has seen a growing literature in Britain that has attempted to address itself to the question of providing an appropriate education for what has been belatedly recognised as a culturally diverse society. Despite this growth, the whole area is still relatively unexplored. As this book was being finished, the most significant official inquiry into this area, *Education for All* the Swann Report (DES, 1985), was published, and revealed only too clearly the relative lack of progress that has been made. British society, and its educational system in particular, still requires major shifts in both policy and practice if the needs of all children are to be even adequately met.

This book examines the context within which education takes place, and more specifically, looks at educational practice to see what has been and can be done to combat the racism that currently permeates much of schooling. Given the range of issues involved, this book attempts to be indicative rather than comprehensive: identifying procedures, policies and practice which demonstrate that education can be a force for change despite the powerful constraints within which it operates.

The book demonstrates two further aspects of work in this area. The first is that there is no one perspective on how to bring about the changes that are so clearly needed. All the contributors are committed to a belief that racism, like sexism, is endemic in education itself and that many educational practices should be changed, but within this general position, there are differences in emphasis which are reflected in their contributions. For example, the contributors share the view that the issues arising from racism and cultural diversity which provide the greater part of the content of this book are crucially interrelated with issues of class and gender. They differ considerably, however, in the extent to which they articulate these interconnections in their papers.

The second aspect is closely related to the first, and that is that there is no optimum to be aspired to. The British educational system is itself extremely complex and diverse. What is effective in one context may well be ineffective in another. The interweaving of context, theory and practice informs the basic structure of the book. In the first chapter, Jagdish Gundara places the whole debate in its broader context, looking at how British society, like others, has always been culturally diverse. The educational consequences of this are examined and the recent upsurge in activity, particularly in policy at national and local level is described and commented on. Crispin Jones's chapter is complementary to Gundara's. The attention here is more sharply on the nature of racism within British society and the comparative failure of education to tackle it effectively. The third chapter, by Peter Fraser, examines these issues more closely, this time specifically from the perspective of the black groups in British society. In the fourth chapter, Eigil Pedersen brings down the focus more sharply on the classroom in a detailed examination of the way in which teachers affect (positively or negatively) the life chances of their pupils. The consequence of such actions for black children is clearly demonstrated. The burgeoning growth of post-sixteen provision, and its differential impact on black young people is the theme of the next chapter, by Godfrey Brandt. He argues that, far from enhancing such young people's opportunities, these new structures are diminishing them and need, therefore, to be examined much more critically and, if necessary, confronted and opposed.

A general paper on the school curriculum introduces the succeeding papers. In this Keith Kimberley emphasises the extent of the re-thinking necessary if all students are to be given access to an understanding of the world in which they live and encouraged to participate actively within it. The paper by Tom Vassen which follows looks specifically at a 'whole school policy' within six primary schools. He describes the outcomes of the policy and discusses the implications of the work undertaken for in-service provision, parental involvement, and Local Education Authority (LEA) support. At a more specific level, Celia Burgess describes a sequence of work in the primary classroom in which children, teachers and parents are all involved in an anti-racist and anti-sexist stance. The children's and the parents' views are included as well as an analysis of the work's content. Terry Mears considers the ways in which the secondary science curriculum will need to be re-thought if it is to meet the needs of a society which recognises itself as multicultural and seeks to be anti-racist. The paper criticises the narrowness of much school science and offers alternative perspectives. Finally, there is an important paper in which resources and library provision are discussed by Gillian Klein who focuses on the contribution to change which can be achieved through new approaches to resource provision and a reassessment of the function in school of the librarian.

The contributors are researchers, academics, teacher trainers, practising teachers and a librarian, who have been associated with the Centre for Multicultural Education at the University of London Institute of Education in various capacities. This collaborative and cooperative exercise attempts to bridge the gaps between those who teach in schools and those who train the teachers.

The Swann Report (DES, 1985) marks an opportunity for the DES and all LEAs, examination boards, colleges and schools to make the dimensions discussed in this book central to future thinking about schooling and the curriculum. It also provides an impetus for programmes of curriculum development to be initiated at a variety of levels, including the DES, the School Curriculum Development Committee and the Secondary Examination Council. Whether sufficient resolve will be found to take on the complex, major reconceptualisation involved and whether the necessary resources for curriculum development, teacher training and research will be provided, remains to be seen. For both resolve and resources will be needed to achieve for all students an education which combines international and multicultural perspectives with a commitment to tackling racism in all its forms.

We would like to thank Diane Nair and Elaine Haydon for help in the book's preparation. Finally, we would especially like to thank our colleague, Godfrey Brandt, who gave us great help at a crucial stage in the putting together of the book.

1 Education for a Multicultural Society

Jagdish Gundara

In this introductory chapter an attempt will be made to cover a broad canvas of issues relating to 'multiculturalism' as they impinge on various debates about education. Many of these debates continue to take place despite the lack of agreement about nomenclature. Words like 'multicultural', 'multiethnic' and 'multiracial', which are all widely used, are commonly ill-defined. Furthermore, theoretical concepts in this field are few and those that have been proposed are often either not accessible to teachers or else are without a broad consensus about their relevance to the teaching profession.

The recent upsurge of interest and activity in 'multicultural education' is part and parcel of larger questions about education within its social context. This context is both national and international and recognises increasing interdependence in the world. Many people, especially those of the younger generation, are becoming acutely conscious of the enormous gaps which exist between the rich and the poor, black and white. They are aware of the precarious nature of their own personal futures and the disparity between current rhetoric on environmental conservation and the stockpiling of weapons of ultimate destruction. Crucial, for them as for the societies in which they live, is the resolution of issues of diversity and uniformity within the nation state. They seem particularly conscious of the urgency of the crisis within and between the nation states. Young people in Britain are as concerned with these issues as are those in other parts of the world.

The economic recession has led to massive youth unemployment and, within that group, particularly black[1] youth. Combined with specific government policies, it has also affected the amount of money devoted to many local and national services. Although education in particular has suffered, the recession has also adversely affected much of the total social environment.

A further aspect of the social context which is relevant is an increasing concern over issues of social order. Crime rates are used like religious texts to demonstrate the moral decline of the nation. The urban uprisings in Brixton and Toxteth during 1981 were also presented as symptomatic of such a general (that is, moral) decline. However, both the claims about crime rates and the suggestion of moral decline as the cause of urban unrest are strongly contested. The state has made a determined effort to play down or ignore the element of racism in these events and to acknowledge the involvement of white youth. Similar blindness has affected much of the examination of police/public relations. The widespread distrust of the police within many black communities has still to be tackled properly.

Poor police/community relations are, however, but one aspect of the racism that seems endemic in much of British society and its institutions. The fluctuating electoral fortunes of the Fascist parties in recent years are one obvious manifestation. More worrying has been the continuous refusal by many sections of the population to see Britain as a society within which black people have a place. The 1981 Nationality Act is an example of this. Similarly, the patriotic fervour that it was possible to invoke and manipulate in relation to the conflict in the South Atlantic gave an indication of the extent to which ethnocentric views still dominate the way in which the majority population views the world.

Within a climate that appears so hostile to improving race relations, it is not surprising that education has been so slow in responding effectively to the challenges posed by schooling in and for a multicultural society. The dominant shift of political forces has been towards the Right in recent British political and social life. This in turn has evoked resistance by the working class and the black community. Similarly, the women's movement has brought about a number of shifts in institutional structures and within the social fabric. The resistance of the black community is nowhere more apparent than in education.

Changes in the Societal Context: Redefining Nationality

As a descriptive term, 'multicultural society' continues to be useful since it points towards diversity as a feature of British society in historical and contemporary terms. Britain's historical diversity on the basis of language, religion, social class and territorial grouping is an established fact. The immigration of visibly different communities has highlighted this aspect of racism which previously had implications for the Celtic, Jewish and travelling communities. Differential power arrangements in society affect all these groups.

Institutions and structures of the state reshape and mould the various features of diversity in British society. The processes, mechanisms and reasons why and how these diversities operate tend to be underplayed as does their effect on education. These processes require considerable critical analysis since the nation state, for various reasons, may at times wish to stress its sovereignty and unity and underplay its social diversity. Similarly, the stress on immigrants and 'ethnicity' may help in diverting attention away from the broader questions of national minorities, as well as from major problems such as racism.

As the immigrants have become more settled in Britain there has been a concern about defining their legal and political position within British society. The most common designation has been that of 'ethnic minorities'. However, this is not a satisfactory term since the new settlers, by and large, have basic problems of nationality and citizenship in Britain which are unrelated to ethnicity. The new settlers in Britain have come from other nation states and most of these states also have diverse populations. These settlers are therefore either nationals of the country of origin or of the country of settlement. Their position in legal and political terms is continually being undermined through immigration and nationality legislation. This legislation is racist in its intent and not directed against the 'ethnicity' of the settlers. As and when these groups resist racism in Britain, they do not do so on the basis of 'ethnic' solidarity, but as Turkish or Greek nationals, or as blacks in Britain. Since the new settlers live in the British nation state and the concept of citizenship is not defined in terms of their 'ethnicity', it may be useful to reappraise the use of this term. The use of 'ethnicity' by social anthropologists has not helped in clarifying this complex issue because they have often ignored the study of aspects of English ethnicity and nationality. It is necessary for those involved with such issues to undertake a more systematic analysis of the basis of the British nation state in historical and contemporary terms so that a clear definition may emerge. For instance, what are the differences between the national minorities and 'ethnic' minorities? Do the national minorities (say, in Scotland and Wales) accept the British nation state as defined by the dominant ruling class? There is, furthermore, a need to define the nature of British society and its relationship to the structures of the nation state.

Since the national minorities occupy different positions within the nation state, the settlers are similarly faced with differing definitions by this state. Different status is accorded to the new settlers based on different realities. To a certain extent the terms 'immigrant' or 'ethnic minority' (which have negative connotations in Britain) may be considered an improvement in a country like West Germany which considers itself a 'non-immigration' country.

Certain national minorities in Britain and the rest of Europe have a territorial basis (Scotland, Wales, Corsica) which are constitutionally recognised within the state. However, the newly-settled communities also occupy urban spaces which may not be constitutionally recognised by the nation states but nevertheless represent the birth of new communities. The black community, as part of the working class, lives in communities like Brixton, Southall and Handsworth which form 'sanctuaries' against the racism which they experience.

The more oppressive the nation states become in their attitude towards the settled and the national minorities, the more likely there will emerge alliances between various oppressed groups. In Britain those who become conscious of racism, sexism and class oppression are likely to consider alliances on the basis of these oppressions.

The oppressive measures also lock the oppressed groups in forms of resistance and change which not only question their own positions but all the structures and apparatus of the state. Hence what emerge in journals like *Race and Class* are fundamental critiques of the British capitalist state. Such critiques demand a rigorous analysis and restructuring of the societies in which the oppressed groups live.

Changes in the General Educational Context

Alongside these wide-ranging changes in society, there are significant recent developments in the national educational context. These can be referred to here only in the briefest manner but it seems important to recognise that they form the backdrop for much of the discussion that follows, both in this chapter and in later ones.

The current economic crisis has had its consequences for educational provision. The strict imposition of cash limits on local government spending has made the choices of those responsible for education in the county halls increasingly difficult. Those who have agreed to make major cuts in expenditure have found themselves choosing between such items as books, teachers, building maintenance, and the meals service; sometimes being obliged to cut back drastically in all areas. Those who have made some cuts but have also attempted to maintain the curriculum and a reasonable level of resource provision, are now, at the time of writing, to be forced into equally hard decisions by means of government legislation to limit local government power in raising money through the rates. In these circumstances, it is not surprising that only a very small amount of money is being made available for such priorities as in-service courses and secondment, new curriculum developments, and projects requiring specialist appointments or generous teacher/student ratios.

This financial stringency also corresponds with a downturn in the number of secondary students – a consequence of a substantial decline in the birth rate. This has made necessary much secondary reorganisation and the process of amalgamation and reshaping of provision has still to work its way through to sixth-form level. It is a time of stress and uncertainty for teachers and institutions: teachers by virtue of the need to apply for jobs in compromise amalgamations, and institutions in relation to the creation of stability and structures which work for the benefit of the majority. In a small number of cases, amalgamation has been seen as an opportunity for creating a new curriculum and developing a new sense of purpose, but for many it appears to have been a dispiriting experience, with retrenchment the order of the day.

At the same time, education has continued to be subject to ideological onslaught. Images of schooling, both fictional and documentary, in the media and news reports, all suggest poor schooling as the cause of many of the wider social ills: lack of social cohesion, 'inadequate' orientation to the world of work/ unemployment; equally programmes and articles accuse teachers of inculcating 'value-free ideologies' or left-wing views. Part of this attack is a later phase of the 'Black Paper' concern for 'standards' institutionalised by central government in certain key forms. One is the maintenance of the view that independent schools represent the best education available. This is being maintained by the use of public funds to ensure that the 'brightest' students are encouraged to attend them and are financed through the Assisted Places Scheme. Another is the requirement that all schools publish their examination results with its side effects that schools in different circumstances defensively concentrate on the success of such students as are seen likely to get top grades and spend a great deal of energy on promoting the image of the school. Lastly, the Assessment of Performance Unit (APU) trundles on along its way testing its 25 per cent quota of students in various subjects each year.

A dissatisfaction with schools and the efforts of teachers seems to lie behind the most drastic piece of central government intervention which is the extension of the role of the Manpower Services Commission (MSC) to cover an extremely wide range of educational provision. It is clear that as from March 1984 the responsibilities of the MSC are to cover all provision for vocational education and training. What this means is that the Department of Employment (DoE), rather than the DES, is now responsible for significant areas of education which, traditionally, have been located in colleges of further education and schools. The White Paper of 1981 (DoE, 1981) established the government's intention to improve the preparation of school and college students for working life; to modernise apprenticeship and other occupational training; and to provide an increased number of training opportunities for adults. The White Paper of 1984 proposes the pattern of a technical and vocational education initiative (TVEI) for fourteen to eighteen year olds, seventeen plus pre-vocational courses for sixth form and colleges (CPVE) as well as the Youth Training Scheme (YTS) (DES/DoE, 1984).

Alongside these changes, an unreformed Advanced-level system is to be maintained as the élite route to university and the professions, though there are proposals for some modification of the over-specialisation of many A-level students through the introduction of Advanced Supplementary Level. Thus post-sixteen students will either: follow A and AS-level courses; be routed into technical and business courses which are pre-vocational; or be offered places on the YTS. Some will be continuing courses under the TVEI scheme or undertaking fully-fledged vocational courses. The pattern underlying this evolution is therefore emerging as a tripartite division: academic, technical and training.

The institutional divisions which seem likely to follow from

these shifts in control of the curriculum and assessment may
have important implications for students from groups which are
subject to various forms of discrimination in society. Evidence
from other European countries with broadly similar divisions,
suggests that the children of immigrant families tend to be
concentrated in low-status routes through education and
training. For example, highly developed systems of vocational
preparation, in both France and the Federal Republic of
Germany, appear to have proved inadequate to meet the
demands placed on them by students from immigrant minority
groups. Second and subsequent generations appear to be
disproportionately represented in those sections of the educational system conferring the most restricted life chances.[2]

Alongside these changes in the structure of educational
provision, a substantial review of the secondary and primary
school curriculum and the means by which it is assessed has
been undertaken. This includes far-reaching shifts in the
control of the curriculum and examinations which disrupt the
traditional pattern of devolution of responsibility for the
curriculum to the LEAs. Moves are being made simultaneously
on several fronts. First, central government has made its own
official statement in *The School Curriculum* (DES, 1981b) and
has institutionalised criteria by which the sixteen plus examination syllabuses of the new General Certificate of Secondary
Education are to be judged. The plans of the Secretary of State
to move away from exams in which students are judged relative
to each other require a further refinement of 'grade specific'
criteria against which they can in future be judged. Another
current development is the specification of objectives for
primary and early secondary education in some subjects. This
assertion of a stronger central control of the curriculum and
assessment is now a well-established feature of the educational
landscape, though it is as yet unclear as to whether, in the
rhetoric of the 'partnership' proposed by Sir Keith Joseph, the
details of curricular practice are now to be dictated from the
centre, or whether substantial room for manoeuvre is still to be
left for LEAs and schools.

Those engaged with education at national, local and institutional levels, particularly teachers, have not only to cope with
such general and specifically educational issues as those sketched
out above, but also to engage with the conceptual and
practical challenge posed by the increasing recognition that *all*
students should be educated for living in a multicultural society.

Anti-racism and Multiculturalism in Education

To describe the necessary provision for all students to be educated for living and participating fully in society, the terms 'anti-racist' and 'multicultural' have been used extensively. These terms have largely superseded earlier terminology like 'multi-racial' and 'multi-ethnic'. Despite its broader terms of reference, the word 'multicultural' has itself recently been subject to a variety of criticisms. It has been censured as being marginal to the mainstream educational debate since it did not deal with the substantive educational issues. These detractors have argued that many teachers use it uncritically to 'celebrate cultures' in schools and are therefore unable to come to grips with basic issues of power and oppression in society. They stress that there have tended to be dichotomies created between discourses on broad educational issues and those concerning 'multicultural education', as if these discourses are somehow separate. It has also been pointed out that issues relating to the curriculum and knowledge systems have tended to be detached from the connections between knowledge and power.

Another set of criticisms of the term 'multicultural' is based on the grounds that its history is embedded in a deficit or disadvantage mode of analysing the black community and this has tended to pathologise them. These criticisms stress that the practices associated with multiculturalism are grounded in the argument that its use by institutions of the state (like the DES and LEAs) is essentially concerned with the containment of black resistance to schooling.[3]

The term 'multicultural society' however, still appears to be useful in describing a broad range of diversity within a society, e.g. linguistic, religious, class and gender, which are all relevant to the process of education. It is, furthermore, inclusive of both ways of living and underlying power relations. Education for a multicultural society is seen as education providing students with means of understanding all the elements in a society in which they are growing up.

'Anti-racism' both specifies a key element in the analysis of British society in that racism is embedded in our interpersonal relations, in our ideology and in our institutions, and also adopts a moral and political stance towards it. The associations of the term 'racist' have sometimes made it difficult for teachers to relate their own practices to demands that they should adopt an anti-racist stance – how could anyone suggest that they are racist?

Wasn't racism what Hitler did to the Jews? Another difficulty, perhaps more theoretical than practical, lies in the way in which acceptance of the term 'anti-racism' might be thought of as an acceptance of a biological concept of 'race'; though, of course, 'anti-racism' is defined explicitly in terms of resistance to behaviour and beliefs of those people who have held that such a concept could justify treating some human beings as inferior to others.

The great advantage of the anti-racist approach has been that it has broken through discussions about racialism and questions of whether people's attitudes towards each other could be made more harmonious through education, to an analysis of institutional arrangements by which one group's schooling and access to the curriculum may offer more limited life chances than others.

National Policy

National policy in the whole area of multiculturalism and anti-racist education has been particularly lacking in any consistency or direction. It has furthermore involved little consultation with the black community on the issues of racism in education. In general terms, there has been a shift from discussions about assimilation to those of cultural pluralism, but this shift is only a benevolent recognition of diversity. There is also a large gap between the declared policies and the practice of such policies, since official rhetoric has not been reflected in schools. There is a widening gap between the national policy-makers and bureaucrats and the black community who have seen a few generations of their children being failed by the education system. Nor has the official discourse included the substantive issues raised by the parent groups and teachers' organisations.[4]

In the 1960s the presence of the black community was largely seen as having created 'problems' within the education system. Hence in 1963 the first formal advice from the DES to the LEAs concerned the issue of the basic language needs of children who needed to speak English to be integrated into the system. Two years later, in 1965, the DES was recommending dispersal. In Circular 7/65 the DES asserted that, as the proportion of immigrant children increased, the problems would become more difficult to solve and the chances of assimilation more remote. The DES was concerned with not offending white parents, and its dispersal policy was based on the premise that language difficulties of immigrant children impeded the learning of white children.

The DES only began to change its policies in the 1970s and started to talk about 'this country's multicultural society'. By the time the 'great debate' took place in 1976, the implications for the curriculum of social diversity had to be mentioned because of the pressure on the DES (DES, 1977). *The School Curriculum* (DES, 1981b) also reflected this pressure. This document, however, failed to stress that British society is fundamentally and historically diverse and the visibility of the black community was only one dimension of that social diversity. It also did not acknowledge the nature of problems posed for education by knowledge being filtered through an Anglocentric view of the world, including its imperial past and neocolonial present. It should also have discussed issues of endemic racism in British society, but since it was a token response, it was made in terms of the visible black community and hence was totally inadequate.

Implementation of policies was initiated at the national level by allocating funds through Section 11 of the Local Government Act, 1966. Funds made available through the Act enabled the local education authorities to claim 75 per cent grant from the Home Office towards the salaries of staff employed to work in areas where there were over 2 per cent 'immigrants'.

Even in this period of immigration when immigrants were defined as coming from the 'New Commonwealth', there was no concerted strategy to deal with special needs. Despite the shift in the rhetoric of the DES about multiculturalism, the use of Section 11 funding through the Home Office remains the government's major intervention in education as far as the black community is concerned. In terms of the broader questions and issues posed for education by the fundamental diversities in British society, the DES has taken no firm action.

A National Foundation for Educational Research (NFER) study in 1971 (Townsend, 1971) described the government's provision as patchy and uneven, particularly since some LEAs gave low priority to educational issues in multiracial areas. The Parliamentary Select Committee on Race Relations and Immigration in 1973 criticised the inadequate provision for immigrant children as well as the lack of consideration of the wider implications for a multicultural society. The DES was extremely wary of implementing any recommendations, including ones for a special fund, because it would reduce the scope of local responsibility.

The DES responded to the Select Committee by accepting the need for examining the results of racial disadvantage. This was done by setting up a Committee of Inquiry. The Rampton Committee was set up in 1979 to give an 'early and particular attention' to the needs of West Indians, and it made an Interim Report in 1981 (DES, 1981a). The DES held 'wide consultations' on this Report but did not take any practical action. At the time of writing, the Swann Report (DES, 1985) confirms that what has to be done still needs 'early and particular attention' and the responses of the DES are awaited.

Partly as a consequence of the general lack of central direction from the DES, structural problems have emerged at the LEA level. For instance, English-as-second-language teams and centres had been set up to deal with the language needs of 'immigrants'. With the shift to broader multicultural policies, these teams and centres were being expected to take on the wider curriculum needs of a multicultural school without being given the staffing or training to make this shift. What should, perhaps, have been temporary structures have become more permanent because issues were not perceived in more dynamic terms by education authorities. An Inner London Education Authority (ILEA) Report on Multi-ethnic Education in 1977 asserted: 'Just as there must be no second-class citizens, so there must be no second-class educational opportunities' (ILEA, 1977). Since the second-class status in terms of both citizenship and educational opportunities continues to exist, it ought to be a matter of national concern. The issue is further compounded because the differences in equality of outcomes have widened within the educational institutions as well as in the world outside the school. There also exist gaps between the expectations of the black parents and children and their experiences which inform the responses of the black community to the education system. The generation of parents which migrated to Britain had very high expectations of the educational system. These have not been met in the experiences of their children, who in turn refuse to accept the low status accorded to them inside and outside the school. The DES policies have viewed the presence of black children in schools as a problem, which has thus lent legitimacy to the dominant mono-cultural view of schooling. Attitudes and policies of the DES have also compounded the problems in British education by not dealing with the special needs of the black community during the 1960s and 1970s. As this community has become more settled in Britain the DES has lost an opportunity fundamentally to reappraise the education of all children in this country. The lack of initiative at the national level has led to an extremely uneven response to issues of diversity in education by the LEAs.

Local Education Authority Policies

In some areas where the black community has settled, the LEAs took initiatives to deal with issues as they saw appropriate. Some of these earlier policy statements in the field of multiculturalism were very much related to the presence of 'ethnic' groups. The ILEA policy document referred to above, in 1977 attempted to come to terms with the presence in London schools of immigrant children from the 'New Commonwealth'. Provision was made to tackle language needs of the children and the ILEA's Unified Language Teaching Service has been strengthened through the years.

As the Authority has acquired more experience in various areas and realised that the 1977 policy document has only marginally affected the educational performance of all children, including black children, there has been a succession of initiatives which have extended into wider issues of the education system, culminating in a major set of ideological and institutional measures to tackle diverse problems. Some authorities (Haringey, Brent, ILEA, Berkshire, Birmingham) have directed resources into reviewing and regenerating areas of the curriculum. Advisory and inspectorate staff have been established. Teachers have been seconded to develop curriculum materials, and links with the community have been developed. In certain authorities where the English-as-second-language provision continues to be the focus, the wider changes have not been instituted. The language issue, however, seems to have been extended with the provision of some classes for teaching of mother tongues.

The provision of advanced teaching of languages in the classroom and language work within the specialist subjects has still remained largely inadequate. So, too, have language issues related to the status of Asian languages as Modern languages and also the issue of Afro-Caribbean languages in the context of the mainstream curriculum.

In authorities such as Haringey and Brent, where the concerns have broadened through practice and political decisions, updated policies on education for a multicultural society, as distinct from 'multicultural education', have been developed. There is increasing evidence that, within the work of these authorities, the idea of educating all children for life in a multicultural society is being used to confront issues of oppression, to bring together in a general framework broad educational issues in 'multicultural education' and to make connections between power relationships in society and the curriculum as a part of this social construct. Others, like Berkshire and ILEA, have adopted policies on racism where issues of gender, class and race are being addressed (Berkshire, 1982; ILEA, 1983). These LEAs are pinpointing inequality as the key issue which needs to be addressed in bringing about social justice.

The Rampton Report (DES, 1981a) has acknowledged the issue of racism as it may affect educational achievement. A few of the LEAs, particularly where 'West Indian underachievement' is a major phenomena, have not been able to ignore the subject. Hence, issues beyond those of teaching standard English have had to be taken account of by some LEAs. The Waltham Forest Authority has been engaged in merging the West Indian Support Service and the English as Second Language Service into a centralised, multicultural development service which can address the issues within the mainstream. This marks a shift from their earlier structures which were clearly modelled on notions of compensatory education.

Some of the LEAs also could not ignore the uprisings of 1981 which had resulted from decades of racial inequality and discrimination. However, policy documents are in themselves no evidence of anti-racist practices, and only the ILEA and Berkshire seem to have taken on board the issues raised by institutionalised and structural racism.

Once certain authorities enact policies which need to be assessed, the problem of monitoring the policies has to be confronted. No general agreement exists on this because many members of the black community do not agree with the proposal to collect more information and statistics about their community. They fear the concentration of a vast amount of information about them in the hands of government departments which they feel operate discriminatory legislation and practices against them. This issue has been discussed in various local authorities.[5]

In 1981, the ILEA decided on a sophisticated form of monitoring of opportunities and grouping of pupils. It also decided to make an agreement with unions and other organisations to monitor jobs for black teachers.

The whole issue of home-school links also seems to have shifted ground. While in the past the aim was to inform the parents about the role of the education service, there has now been a shift so that in authorities like the ILEA and Brent, the home and the school can ensure mutual support and information, including the resources within the community. However, a critical perspective on the nature and importance of home-school links is needed since many current practices are based on untested assertions.

Many LEAs' practice suggests that changes relating to the curriculum are a result of the presence of the pupils of New Commonwealth origin. This was particularly true in the area of the Humanities. The ILEA's work on the Reading Through Understanding Project and the World History Project are two examples of such work. Certain curriculum areas like mathematics and sciences have been slow to receive attention but need closer scrutiny because of the underachievement of girls and working-class children in these subjects. Brent is an example of an authority which has devised a policy for all pupils based on issues of knowledge and curriculum in these broader terms (Brent, 1983). However, the implementation of this policy depends on the political will within the authority being accompanied by appropriate changes in the authority's structures and school practices.

At another level, there are gaps between policy and practice because the LEA structures and institutions themselves are resistant to change. In some authorities multicultural advisers are peripheral to the mainstream of advisers and inspectors. Their marginalisation detracts from the influence and power they need to bring to bear to implement any changes in the mainstream practices of the authority and schools. For example, the ILEA is in the process of implementing a report on the organisation and curriculum of secondary schools, *Improving Secondary Schools.*[6] This report makes a wide range of recommendations which include issues of a bilingual and multicultural nature. There may be problems, however, in carrying out the recommendations because the report does not suggest optimum 'multicultural' or 'anti-racist' practices and means for their development and implementation at all levels of the education system.

Similarly in schools, multicultural and anti-racist policies may not have the support of the entire staff, particularly if these are not based on consultation with all sections of the school community. If the schools were to implement policies to change structures and practices which were racist without some certainty about outcomes, then the result would be variable across the country. The uneven and patchy changes brought about in institutions do not give credence to real commitment to equality in education for all children.

Many teachers and advisers who have been working towards instituting changes to bring about equality feel that institutional and LEA-based measures are not enough. They consider that it is necessary to have a concerted national strategy to deal with inequality resulting from racism. These teachers particularly feel this to be the case because facile statements about multiculturalism based on 'celebration of cultures' has not included a critical appraisal of knowledge and culture.

Language Issues in Education

The emphasis on language issues has mainly revolved around the issue of teaching English as a second language (ESL). From the earliest years it has been considered that children who spoke languages other than English as first languages only needed to acquire competence in English. The mechanisms to ensure this have included reception classes as well as the provision of language centres to teach ESL. The basic premise has been to integrate and assimilate these children into the mainstream English society which itself remained undefined. This, however, meant that children of Afro-Caribbean origin were considered to be speakers of English and no account was taken of issues related to dialect or Creole speakers. The policies of concentrating on the teaching of ESL, to the exclusion of children's mother tongues, in units outside the mainstream classrooms, and of ignoring dialect and Creole issues, have depressed the educational potential of subsequent generations of children of the black community. The potential of multilingualism and bilingualism has been lost for a few generations of youth and that of developing the first languages of children has been negated. While some parents may have accepted the dominance of English and not stressed first languages of their children, many sections of the community have set up community schools to teach these languages on a voluntary basis. An emphasis on learning ESL has left a legacy of structures, and a cadre of ESL teachers has determined the issue of language teaching in a one-dimensional way. This domination of debate by English has left a legacy of lost opportunities, partly because of the way in which the parents have perceived the usefulness of English as a dominant language. Jane Miller illustrates this with the following example:

> Kulvinder is five and halfway through her first year of primary school. Her teacher sometimes feels concerned that Kulvinder doesn't speak at school, but she lets herself be reassured by the child's bright watchfulness and by the alacrity with which she always does what she's told. Besides, Kulvinder's mother and father are so keen for their daughter to speak good English that they have given up speaking Punjabi at home and speak only English now. Kulvinder doesn't say much at home either, but perhaps that will change when her parents have learned more English themselves (Miller, 1983).

This issue, however, is not so simple because the ESL programmes set up for adults have on the whole failed except for those who wanted to enter the employment market. Many parents have not learnt 'survival English' and the gaps between them and their children who only speak English have increased enormously. The ill-thought-out and haphazardly implemented ESL provison for adults, which included a combination of statutory and voluntary provision, has not succeeded in its object of teaching men and women English. Mothers in particular have become alienated from English society as well as from their children. This has also reinforced their working-class positions within British society. The main points of contact within the family remain the hostility that parents and children feel because of racism. There has developed a community solidarity which uses customs, traditions and religion to protect the community against incursions from institutions outside the home. This siege mentality seems to have protected the community from enforced change by the dominant community, but has not allowed the interaction and development of home languages and cultures alongside those of the more powerful English society. As a consequence, many children are only bilinguals orally since they do not possess writing skills and overall competence in the first language. The community languages, however, do continue to survive in various forms.[7]

The structural problems posed by special language units are considerable and major work needs to be undertaken so that the role of children's languages in the mainstream curriculum can be established in a systematic manner. This perspective is supported by numbers of ESL teachers.[8] That relocation of English as second language within the curriculum will need to be undertaken at all levels of the schooling process and by all the subject teachers has recently been highlighted by the setting up a working party on language awareness by the Royal Society of Arts and by work done in languages at many schools, including the North Westminster Community School in London. This support for bilingualism is illustrated by the chart opposite designed by the former Schools Council Mother Tongue Project.[9]

The implications for teachers and teacher trainers appear to be quite profound. This is particularly so if the issues of languages are not to be examined and dealt with in tokenistic terms.[10] Monolingual teachers need to engage in discussions with the community on the ways and means by which bilingual pupils can be taught alongside monolingual pupils (Brent, 1983). The pupil as a resource in the classroom can be supplemented by the bilingual community outside the school.

There are, however, other structures and issues that now dictate the debate. The first is the growth of supplementary language instruction which goes on outside the schools. The second is the use of first languages by young blacks as a language of resistance. Both of these entail a hardening of the positions within the black community on issues of education. Negotiations about teaching languages within the school and the use of the community as a resource will most probably entail positive action by the educational establishment. Black parents and students appear no longer willing to allow a tokenistic involvement with schools unless they can see the context and shift in the education system as a whole. Language policies which emerge as a result of a broader strategy and action may provide the basis for involving the community. Because of the broad range of oppressive measures, including linguistic oppression, a marginalised involvement in the future is certain to be rejected by the black community.

Black Responses to Educational Policies

The black community does not currently possess power equal with that of the dominant white community, and because of the

WHY SUPPORT BILINGUALISM?

Benefits for *all children:*

1 Supports confidence in own language repertoire
2 Increases language awareness
3 Contributes to combating racism
4 Increases awareness of cultural diversity
5 Increases communication between different cultural groups

Benefits for *bilingual children:*

1 Support for learning
2 Aiding intellectual/ cognitive development
3 Supporting self-esteem/ confidence in own ethnicity*
4 Supporting relationship with family and community
5 Extending vocational and life options

BASIC PRINCIPLES

1 Equality of opportunity
2 Developing skills and talents that children bring to school
3 Responding positively to a multicultural society

Benefits for *the teacher* and *the school:*

1 Increases knowledge of and relationship with individual pupils
2 Recognition of pupils' family/ community as a resource
3 Increases teacher awareness of linguistic and cultural diversity
4 Strengthens school/community links
5 Contributes to multicultural ethos of the school

* The term 'linguistic community' may be more helpful here. (J.G)

increased institutionalised racism of the British state, has at each stage rejected the state's oppressive and exclusive policies towards its presence in British society. This institutionalised racism exists on the statute books by virtue of discriminatory Immigration Acts and the Nationality Act 1981. It also exists in the shape of the customs and practices of various institutions dealing with housing, health, education and employment. Pressure from the black community to examine and scrutinise policies and practices has resulted in acknowledgment of discriminatory practices and the need to deal with these, although measures to readdress these at various levels appear to have been minimal.

While the Caribbean, African and South East Asian immigrants came from different parts of the world to Britain, they brought a common understanding of the British society. That is the fact that they had experienced British colonial oppression and had been party to the political liberation movements and struggles in the colonies. Those who were born in Britain had learnt from their parents and from their own experiences of British racism. The historical dimension of black resistance to oppression is therefore of fundamental importance. As Stuart Hall writes:

> The indigenous racism of the '60s and '70s is significantly different, in form and effect, from the racism of the 'high' colonial period. It is a racism 'at home' not abroad. It is the racism not of a dominant but of a declining social formation (Hall, 1978).

The clarity with which the blacks see racial oppression in Britain today as having its roots in the colonial experience, has led to their refusal in class terms to assimilate on the basis of language, culture and religion. The clearer their refusal to assimilate and integrate appears to be, the more clearly their refusal has pointed to the diversities and inequalities in British society at large.

In the assimilationist period, the racist institutional practices remained invisible and the issues of streaming, dispersal and the educationally subnormal (ESN) continued to operate. The Haringey Black Parents' Group, among others, began to consider educational issues as they concerned black children and their future in Britain. The Caribbean Education and Community Workers' Association through the research of Bernard Coard made an intervention in the education debate by questioning the concept of special education.

The cumulative effect of these educational disadvantages took place while the racist immigration laws of 1968 and 1971 were being enacted. Government-initiated measures of positive discrimination were seen as tokenistic and politically ineffective to counteract massive social disadvantage. Education measures formed within the period in which cultural pluralism has been the dominant assumption seem to have had some impact on the curriculum, particularly with reference to language and history. However, broader and more relevant curriculum changes have not been undertaken and this situation is seen by the black community to sidetrack students from examination success and as a tactic to avoid confronting institutional racism in school structures. The British state has, however, chosen to ignore the general thrust of demands of the black community for equality and justice in British society.

The compound effect of economic, political, social and educational discrimination led to open resistance by black youth in Bristol, Liverpool and London in 1981. In educational terms, specifically, the black community has categorically rejected the compensatory models and the cultural deprivation theories which attempt to scapegoat them for all the educational ills of British society. At all levels of the community, the school, the LEAs, and the teacher training institutions, all need to reappraise the nature, breadth and scope of the issues raised by the black community which, in turn, relate to the broader diversities and power issues in British society.

The black youth of Britain themselves appear to be rejecting schooling and demanding proper education and this has ramifications for all those involved in reshaping the content and structures of education. Superficial responses by the state to co-opt and defuse the issues have not only failed but appear to perpetuate centralised and tradition-bound solutions which bear no relevance to the contemporary generation of black and white youth in educational institutions. The state cannot operate on stereotypical assumptions about the black community and contemporary society as a whole.

The demands for separate schools and the actual provision of supplementary education embody dual criticisms and concerns about the British education system. On the one hand, parents really do not feel satisfied with the education being provided for their children and have therefore set up supplementary schools to teach languages and curriculum subjects like mathematics, history and religion. These schools reflect concerns about both values and skills which are considered important and are not being taught and learnt in state schools. There are also parents who are demanding separate schools for their children because they do not subscribe to some of the methods used in comprehensive schools. The demand appears to be growing through the '80s as the parents blame the schooling process for the lack of motivation to learn, and for their children's low achievements in school. By contrast, motivation is demonstrated by the same children in supplementary schools.

The main thrust behind demand for separate schools is most probably based on the feeling that black youth has become alienated in the school community which is considered racist, and a desire to provide spaces to nurture them away from its negative effects. The black community has seen the responses of the state and the LEAs in answer to racism as merely cosmetic. Neither the policies, structures nor curriculum in education has changed substantively since the mid-sixties when the black community started organising itself against the inequities of British education. The demands for separate schools mark a culmination of this broad map of disadvantage in educational terms. Ideas about education in a pluralist or multicultural society are seen as being meaningless unless they genuinely eliminate educational inequalities and tackle the power basis of inequality.

The issues of endemic racism in schools are seen by the black community to be deeply entrenched. From their third world context they have seen black teachers successfully train generations of students and professionals, and they are not convinced by British exhortations for equal opportunity for black teachers which are seen to be totally facile without substantive action to provide equality in appointments and promotions. The exhortations for equal opportunities do not seem to fit a situation where there are large numbers of skilled black teachers and black professionals whose skills remain unused.

Demands for separate schools do not appear to be based on the grounds of a superficial analysis of 'ethnic' schools for 'ethnic' groups. Neither is it a question of providing jobs for black teachers discriminated against by the larger system, but it is an attempt to address the basic inequalities of the education system which has not been put to rights. Demands for separate schools arise not because of the 'natural' inclinations of the black community for 'ethnic' schools but because of the discriminatory practices on racial and class bases experienced by it on a continuing basis in Britain.

The black community sees that education for all in the same schools is only valid if a viable comprehensive system operates. However, since voluntary-aided schools and public schools exist alongside comprehensive schools, any talk of education for all becomes meaningless because such a range of schools cannot in fact provide equality in education. Well-endowed public schools are not seen as providing the same education as inner city comprehensive schools.

Demands from the Muslim community for religious and single-sex schools pose issues which have no easy answers. The educational establishment has to concede the principle that both denominational and single-sex schools exist, hence the principle of such schools for Muslims cannot be easily ignored. The Swann Report (DES, 1985) provides no solutions on this issue because it does not address itself to the question of secular education for all children in this society.

The various demands of the black community for separate schools are therefore concentrating attention on the *raison d'être* of all educational institutions. The DES and the LEAs cannot readily provide answers about equality of education when in fact structural changes and re-allocation of resources have not been made in the schooling system.

One of the major directions for change in the schooling system has come from the students and the parents. Their role is either ignored or cursorily dismissed as having no impact because of their refusal to accept the ascribed roles for the community.

One of the fundamental issues parents seem to face is the dual oppression in race and class terms. They have resisted the attempts to enforce the worst features of these dual oppressions. Black women have in particular been subjected to the racist and patriarchal immigration and nationality legislation as well as discrimination in employment. As a category of black women, the Asian women, for instance, have demonstrated that they do not fit into the stereotypical roles of being docile and sub-servient. Their oppression, which is a complex issue, has been ably dealt with elsewhere (Parmar, 1982). However, it does inform the younger generation of the need to stand up for their rights in the schooling process. It furthermore appears import-ant that the struggles and resistance of black men, women and children are critically appraised in the light of their wide-ranging experience in the Third World and in Britain so that their demands and responses to the education system are understood in the clearest possible terms. These parents and children do not respond as 'ethnics' who cannot critically appraise the negative features of the schooling system. Many of the young black British generation born in this country do not want to accept roles which do not provide them with equality with their white peers. They therefore resist inside and outside the school through the use of their languages and cultural values.

The black community, however, cannot resolve fundamental educational problems because of the class basis of British society in which they have little power. Since there are no purely educational problems, there can be no purely educational solutions and a broad range of social realities impinge on education as one area of social policy. One of the major issues which will have to be resolved is that there exist very few pedagogic spaces to provide systematic support for education of black and white working-class children.

Many important matters need to be renegotiated by all the parties involved in the learning process. Teachers face a difficult task in their profession and none of the issues mentioned above will make life easier for them. Parents and students not only need to be consulted but should be positively involved in the process of education.

NOTES

1   The term 'black' is here being used for Afro-Caribbean and Asian communities who are visibly different from the white British community and are at the receiving end of one powerful strand of racism.

2   See for example:
    GUNDARA, J. S., JONES, C. AND KIMBERLEY, K. (July 1982) *The marginalisation and pauperisation of the second generation of migrants in France, the Federal Republic of Germany and Great Britain, relating to the education of children of migrants,* Report submitted to the EEC, Brussels.

3   On pathology and disadvantage issues, see, for instance:
    GUNDARA, J. S. 'Approaches to Multicultural Education', in TIERNEY, J. (1982) *Race Migration and Schooling.* London: Holt Reinhart. On black resistance and schooling, see:
    MULLARD, C. *Racism in Society and Schools: History, Policy and Practice* (1980), Occasional paper No. 1, London: University of London Institute of Education, Centre for Multicultural Education.
    CARBY, H. V. (1982) 'Schooling in Babylon', Centre for Contemporary Cultural Studies, *The Empire Strikes Back,*

London: Hutchinson.
DHONDY, F., BEESE, B., HASSAN, L. (1982) *Black Explosion in British Schools*. London: Race Today Publications.

4 Report of a conference organised by the National Convention of Black Teachers (6 November 1982) at the University of London Institute of Education, 20 Bedford Way, London, WC1H OAL. See particularly, Report of Sessions and Resolutions, pp. 20–3.

5 See for example:
KIRKLEES (1981) *Report of the Inter-Directorate Working Party on Multi-ethnic Kirklees*. Kirklees Local Authority.

6 Dr David Hargreaves was commissioned to consider the curriculum and organisation of ILEA secondary schools with special reference to 'pupils who are underachieving' and 'those who show their dissatisfaction with school by absenteeism or other uncooperative behaviour'. The report, *Improving Secondary Schools*, was published by the ILEA in 1984.

7 See the Report by the Linguistic Minorities Project for the Department of Education and Science (July 1983) *Linguistic Minorities in England*. London: University of London Institute of Education and Tinga Tinga.

8 See WRIGHT, J. (1982) *Bilingualism in Education*. London: Issues in Race and Education Collective.
ISSUES IN RACE AND EDUCATION COLLECTIVE (1982) 'Mother tongue: Politics and Practice', *Issues in Race and Education*, 35.
ISSUES IN RACE AND EDUCATION COLLECTIVE (1983) 'Learning and Language: ESL in the mainstream classroom', *Issues in Race and Education*, 39.

9 Reproduced with the permission of SDCS Publications from *Supporting Children's Bilingualism*, Longman, 1983.

10 The dangers are clearly outlined in:
STONE, M. (1981) *The Education of the Black Child in Britain*. London: Fontana.

2 Racism in Society and Schools

Crispin Jones

If schools are effectively to counter racism it is important to have:

(i) a clear understanding of what the term 'racism' actually means;

(ii) an understanding of how and why racism is built into the institutions (including schools) of our society;

(iii) a model of a culturally diverse society for which the schools should prepare all children;

(iv) a range of strategies to help both teachers and students to counter racism in schools and in the wider society.

A major concern of this book is an exploration of the last two of these points. This chapter examines the other two points, in an attempt to provide a contextual framework within which these strategies and models can be assessed.

Race and Racism

It is a singularly unusual person who has no prejudice, i.e. a pre-judgement or opinion to which a *post hoc* rationalisation may or may not be attached. Common examples would include opinions about food, music and sport. At a first glance many such prejudices seem comparatively harmless. This could, however, be debated, for the aesthetic judgements on which many such views implicitly rest are in turn often reflections of the power relations in a society. This relationship is, however, more explicit if prejudices about race, gender or class are examined. In addition, these prejudiced perceptions are the basis of stereotypes, mainly of a derogatory nature. If such prejudiced beliefs and attitudes shape the way in which people behave, as they often do, that behaviour is likely to be discriminatory. In the case of racial prejudice, the outcome is racial discrimination. Two further points need to be made. Prejudiced beliefs are often strongly held and remain relatively unchanged in the light of conflicting evidence or argument. In addition, particularly in terms of prejudices about groups of people, the prejudice is rarely favourable but is usually unfavourable. Thus racial prejudice is not very susceptible to rational debate, and prejudice against certain groups, for example black people in British society, is usually accompanied by an equally prejudiced preference for other groups, usually white in the British context.

Racial prejudice, however, although seldom intellectually challenged by its protagonists, does not come out of a vacuum. Also, the view that racial prejudice and racial discrimination, often abbreviated to racism, are based on ignorance, is not sufficient. If it were so, all that would be needed would be a touch of Ratty's 'Learn 'em' pedagogy and all would be well. But it is not that simple. Although learning 'em may well be a part of the remedy, this ignorance on which so much can be safely blamed deserves a closer examination. What is clear, however, is that there is much confusion throughout the educational system, as well as in the wider society, about the exact nature of race. This state of affairs is not surprising, as, over the years, the word 'race' has acquired a wide variety of meanings, and, at best, most of them are unhelpful and inaccurate. It is important, consequently, briefly to examine this definitional history.

Principal amongst these definitions are those which seek to prove clear biological differences between human groups based on a biological definition of race. Investigations in this area, ostensibly based upon scientific methodology, were commonplace in the last century and the early part of this. Groups of biologists, physical anthropologists and others were concerned not only in establishing differences, but also with establishing a hierarchy of races. Physical appearance was seen to correlate with intellectual, cultural and moral differences, giving scientific support to the racial prejudice and racial discrimination so widely current in British society at that time.

Such 'scientific' investigations merely confirmed the white English in a set of opinions and practices which had had a long history and which is well documented (Walvin, 1971, 1973; Milner, 1983; Tierney, 1982). Some illustrations will help to demonstrate this. For example, discrimination against, and persecution of Jews is a recurrent feature of British history. Queen Elizabeth I issued a proclamation forbidding further settlement of 'blackamoors' within the City of London. Flemings, Lombards and French Protestants were all received with distrust and even hatred by many of the English they settled amongst. But it was the enslavement of African people to work in the prosperous sugar plantations of the Caribbean which has probably had the greatest effect on English conceptions of race, greater even than the more recent, and by no means dead, imperialistic nationalism which sustained the growth and delayed the ending of the British Empire.

The immense profits that accrued from the slave trade and the sugar plantations on which the slaves lived and died helped to fund the Industrial Revolution in Britain. Its inhumanity was clear, or at least it is clear to us today. At the time there was an equally clear view that if there was exploitation, it was not of humans, or at best, humans of such a low sort that they expected little better. An eighteenth-century biologist, Edward Long, described African slaves in Jamaica as 'bestial, libidinous and shameless as monkeys, or baboons' (quoted in Walvin, 1973, p. 163). The philosophers were little better. Hume, writing at about the same time as Long, stated:

> I am apt to suspect the Negroes, and in general, all the other species of men . . . to be naturally inferior to the whites. There never was a civilised nation of any complexion than white, nor even any individual eminent in action or speculation. No ingenious manufactures amongst them, no arts, no sciences (quoted in Tierney, 1982, p. 17).

Matters improved little in the nineteenth century. An early edition of *Encyclopaedia Britannica* described Afro-Caribbean people as full of, 'idleness, treachery, revenge, cruelty, impudence, stealing, lying, profanity, debauchery, nastiness and intemperance' (quoted in Walvin, op. cit., p. 173). Such a description was intended to mean that Afro-Caribbean people were inferior, to be distrusted and despised. It is also important to remember that these were authoritative statements, not the comments of bigots, i.e. bigots as defined by their contemporaries.

As the century proceeded, science, far from rebutting these views, sustained them, either directly or indirectly. Darwin's theory of natural selection, Spencer's survival of the fittest theory and the newly burgeoning science of physical anthropology all appeared to give scientific justification for dividing up humanity into distinct races. These divisions were based on skin colour and, even more insidious, gave apparently rational justification for regarding the non-white races of the globe as being innately inferior. Thus scientific discussion in this area was rooted in the racism of contemporary scientists and their work confirmed their views and the views of others in the wider society. It is a view well expressed by Francis Dalton, who, while writing on the scientific principles of heredity and after attempting to 'prove' the intellectual inferiority of black people, added this significant comment: 'It is seldom that we hear of a white traveller meeting with the black chief whom he feels to be a better man' (quoted in Milner, 1975, p. 18).

Although the result of such a meeting by the time Dalton wrote this was no longer likely to result in physical enslavement, it usually was followed by incorporation into the British Empire. Livingstone's call for the exploitation of Africa for 'commerce and Christianity' (his ordering of priorities), although initially fuelled by philanthropic motives, quickly led to a view of colonised peoples as being childlike and simple, in need of the helping hand of the white man. The message was reiterated in fund-raising lantern slide shows in church halls up and down the country, in Sunday schools and in the textbooks and fiction read by children. Although the worst excesses of slavery might have ended, many of its supportive and sustaining attitudes continued and were added to and reinforced during the period of imperial expansion, nowhere more enthusiastically than in the schools.

The popular image of Victorian and Edwardian state schools is one of calm industriousness. The children were polite, standards were set and maintained, while outside the classroom windows the sun struggled in vain to set on a glorious magenta Empire. As Gerald Grace (1980) has demonstrated, the reality, particularly in the urban school, was very different. Probably the only reality in such an image is the perception of Empire. It *was* believed in. Jingoism was supported with all the fervour of a moral crusade, and England's patronising assumption of world leadership (and exploitation) was generally accepted. The school curriculum was drenched in it, right from the time a child started school, as the following extract from a poem in a primer illustrates:

D is a Dervish from sunny Soudan
He dances no more his eccentric can-can,
But, trained to our manners, is eagerly fain,
When Britain once calls him, to dance in her train.

E is an English babe, ready to take
The yoke of the world for humanity's sake,
So that everyone knows, be it dreary or bright,
When its England that leads him, the road must be right.

F's a Fijian, her hair like a mop;
Let others spin yarns, *she* can spin like a top!
Now she's winning her way to a place in our nation
By skipping from frenzy to civilisation.

G is a Ghurka – a big little man –
With a lion-heart under his covering of tan.
He's fond of his kukri, his gun and his rice,
If the Empire requires him, it needn't call twice.

H is Hong Kong, with a pig-tail yards long:
(They always wear pigtails in distant Hong Kong!)
Though he laughs, he's not laughed at, he's old and yet new;
They'll be no 'Yellow Peril' while he is True Blue![1]

The disturbing thing about such a piece of verse is that it would
not seem too out of place, at least in terms of its attitudes, in a
classroom today (Ghurka soldiers did fight in the Falklands
conflict in 1982). In other words, although the sun has set on the
Empire, the attitudes and emotions that sustained it in Britain
have continued to shape many people's thoughts and actions.

Moreover, the attitudes confirmed in the classroom were not
exclusively directed overseas. Earlier mention has been made of
the hostility expressed towards minority groups in British
society. A black face may have been unusual outside urban areas,
though not nearly as unusual as our history textbooks might
suggest (cf. File and Power, 1981). But other groups were also
seen as inferior 'races'. In the 1840s a noted observer wrote:

> The worst quarters of all the large towns are inhabited by Irishmen.
> Wherever a district is distinguished for especial filth and especial
> ruinousness, the explorer may safely count upon meeting chiefly
> those Celtic faces which one recognises at the first glance as different
> from the Saxon physiognomy of the native . . . (Engels, 1969,
> p. 123).

The point here is not that the writer associates the Irish with 'filth and especial ruinousness' for indeed he goes on to explain that it is their economic and social oppression that is the cause. The point is that Engels could tell – 'at the first glance' – that the inhabitants were of a particular, easily identifiable, racial group. Such beliefs die hard and the Irish have retained a status in society which is often pejorative, as evinced by Irish 'jokes', and still confirmed by discrimination. It is not that long ago that the sign 'No Irish' could be seen in lodging-house windows in London.

In general, however, hostility to such groups in the main ceases when (or if) their descendants merge into the population at large, so that they can no longer be readily identified and discriminated against. This merging, or 'passing', is not an option open to some more recent groups of immigrants, notably those from the Caribbean and the Indian sub-continent. The idea of 'passing' also begs the question as to whether it is a desirable thing in the first place. How just is a society which grants acceptance only to such people who abandon, in public at least, their language, their religion and their cultural and historical affiliations?

Perhaps one group above all exemplifies the manner in which dominant groups in British society tolerate internal diversity, and that is the Jews. Persecuted, expelled or murdered in the middle ages, their subsequent history has been more a modification of such responses rather than a rejection of them. The immigration of Jews around the turn of the century, fleeing from persecution from countries in central Europe and from Russia, brought a richness into British political, cultural and economic life which has yet to be fully assessed. British tolerance was not very evident to many of them. An MP, Evans Gordon, speaking in 1902 , felt able to state:

> It is only a matter of time before the population becomes entirely foreign . . . the rates are burdened with the education of thousands of children of foreign parents . . . The working classes know that new buildings are erected not for them but for strangers from abroad . . . they see the schools crowded with foreign children and the very posters and advertisements on the walls in a foreign tongue . . . A storm is brewing which, if it be allowed to burst, will have deplorable results (quoted in Foot, 1965, p. 88).

The speech has a familiar contemporary ring. It also, quite explicitly, addresses itself to the economic insecurity of the white working classes, inviting them to identify the 'alien' as the principal cause of such insecurity. Just as 'alien' at that time was a racist code word for Jews, now it is 'immigrant', meaning anyone with a black face in British society.

The response to the presence of Jews is a paradigm for the state of current race relations in this country. Around the turn of the century, the cry was 'they take our jobs, they take our houses', usually first espoused by those comfortably in possession of both. In the 1930s, with the rise of Fascist and anti-Semitic regimes in Europe, a contemporaneously familiar note was sounded, and that was the linking of so-called 'British' tolerance and immigration controls. After Hitler came into power in Germany, German Jews attempted to leave Germany and settle in, amongst other places, Great Britain. This pressure increased after 'Crystal Night' in 1938, when it became clear that the anti-Semitism embodied in Hitler's idea of the German Reich was far more than vituperative rhetoric. The 'tolerant' British response was to allow some in, but to deny access to many others. The reasons were not economic, although there was an economic slump at the time. The reason was that the anti-Semitic feeling in Britain would be fanned if Jewish immigration on any scale were to be countenanced (ibid.). Good race relations, in other words, could only be maintained if visible minorities were allowed to immigrate in very low numbers. The problem lay in British society, but the solution was to blame the victim. Like the Evans Gordon speech, it has a familiar ring. As Charles Husband says of later immigration controls, designed to limit immigration from the Caribbean and Indian subcontinent, 'Since as a nation we cannot condone any increase in racial prejudice, and since an increase in the black population would surely result in more prejudice, then we must resist any pressure to admit more blacks' (Husband, 1975, p. 19).

Advice of a similar nature has been given to women who wish to avoid rape, i.e. women walking alone at night offer temptation to would-be rapists; so women should never go out alone at night. And if they then get raped at home they will no doubt be told that they did not secure efficient enough locks on their doors and windows. Blaming the victim seems an easier policy response than tackling the real roots of the problem.

Despite the evidence of the Holocaust, and even that is doubted by certain extremist elements in British society, anti-Semitism is still alive, and if not exactly flourishing, is still active today. The leaflets distributed by Fascist organisations outside the gates of schools in recent years reveal that together with a preoccupation with black people, a major driving force is still one of anti-Semitism. What is revealing about that is that the leadership of such organisations, despite their own preoccupations, have realised that there is more chance of popular support if they campaign against black minorities rather than British Jews.

In other words, the racial prejudice and discrimination that is seen in society and schools today has a long history, contradicting the view that many white British have of their tolerance towards immigrants and minority groups within the nation. The economic exploitation of slaves and colonial people and its intellectual justifications have merely been transposed to a new, but hardly different set of circumstances, following upon the modest immigration of groups of black people to the United Kingdom over the last thirty or so years.

But although the economic exploitation contingent upon these beliefs has continued, it has been in a more subtle and disguised fashion. A critical element in its continuance has been the comparatively constant belief in the reality of biologically-based racial divisions between human societies. More recent scientific research into this area, well summarised by Professor Rose for the National Union of Teachers (NUT, 1978) indicates that to try to divide human groups up in a scientific manner on the grounds of perceptible biological difference, i.e. based on phenotypes, is impossible. As Bohannan (1966), has claimed, such work reduces anthropology 'to the level of alchemy' (quoted in Tierney, 1982, p. 3). More accurate studies, based on genotypes, come up with results that may be useful to geneticists, but the results are of little use in categorising peoples by their physical appearance. Indeed there are proper questions to ask of such attempts, as to what purpose they serve, and in whose interests.

If there is no scientific foundation for the various traditional racial divisions into which humanity is divided, of what value is the term? The fact is, however, that 'race' *is* a useful term, albeit defined in a different way if we are to tackle racial discrimination in an effective manner. A 'race' (following Van den Berghe, 1967) is defined as a group of people who either see themselves and/or are seen by others as being clearly different from other groups of people because of certain innate and unchangeable physical characteristics.

Racial difference is thus a social construction rather than a biological one, i.e. skin colour is important because we think it is important. In addition, membership of a racial group is permanent – there can be no 'passing' or merging into the majority population – and intergenerational. Finally, it should be noted that even this definition, although perhaps a more accurate representation of social reality, is nevertheless a racist concept, in that most of those who use group definitions based on race usually do so for dubious motives. The first step, therefore, in combating racism is to challenge any concept of 'race' which claims any objectivity.

Much of the racism that is encountered in schools and society at large, however, remains firmly rooted in the outmoded and fallacious concepts of race discussed earlier. In this country this usually expresses itself in the innate superiority of the 'white' race over all others. As a contemporary racist puts it, 'while every race may have its particular skills and qualities, the capacity to govern and lead and sustain civilisation as we understand it lies essentially with the Europeans' (John Tyndall, quoted in Walker, 1977, p. 81).

Statements like that, revealing a continued belief in the innate superiority of the European (i.e. white) race over all others, demonstrates the power the outmoded and discredited concepts of race still have. Many of the views that overt racists hold have a similar basis. The most common of these are:

(i)   There are clear and distinct races, clearly distinguishable from one another on biological, moral, cultural, intellectual and aesthetic grounds.
(ii) These races can be arranged in a clear, and in the main, inflexible hierarchy of worth.
(iii) Racial and geographical boundaries overlap.
(iv) The relative economic positions of the various races in the world are the result of racial difference.

Beliefs such as this, akin to those held by Hitler and his supporters, are easy to recognise and most teachers and others involved in education would dismiss them quickly if stated in such a bald manner. Such extreme views, it is now often claimed, are the preserve of a minority of the population. It would, however, be naïve to assume that in British society a small population of 'misguided' people inspired by racist beliefs was opposed by the vast majority of people, free from any taint of such beliefs. Both opinion and electoral polls in recent years show that these racist views have considerable support, and not just in urban areas where ethnic and racial minorities are concentrated. It is an uncomfortable and disquieting state of affairs. British society has long cherished its tolerant, just and humane image. How this view comes to terms with the facts of racial discrimination, evinced in report after report over the last twenty years, is, on the surface, a major quandary. In housing and employment, two important determinants of life chances, there is abundant evidence (e.g. Smith, 1976) of racial discrimination. It is so widespread that it cannot be simply blamed on the actions of a malevolent few. Over an eight-year period, research by Smith for the Political and Economic Planning Unit (PEP) found evidence of massive racial discrimination throughout society. Two examples of their results exemplify this. Examining a sample of degree-level qualified males, 79 per cent of the white men were in professional or management positions while only 31 per cent of men from minority groups with equal qualifications were. None of the white men with degree-level qualifications had manual jobs, but 21 per cent of the men from minority groups with degree-level qualifications had. Discrimination is also manifest at the point of application for jobs. In carefully prepared experiments, gross discrimination against West Indian and Asian applicants for manual jobs was evident in 48 per cent of the applications. These experiments were carried out before the recent rapid rise in unemployment, so that now, in many inner city areas, young black entrants to the job market find it remarkably difficult to get any job at all. Join to this police harassment, the constant threat of physical attack by members of the white community and the recent changes in the nationality laws, and it is difficult to see how many members of minority racial groups can come to any other conclusion than that Britain is a profoundly racist society.

To sum up: if British institutions appear implicitly or explicitly racist, why is so little being done? A public policy commitment to 'racial harmony' appears a meaningless response, implying as it does the idea that benevolence and consideration can end this state of affairs. As writers like Castles and Kosack (1973) have indicated, the position of racial and other comparatively recently arrived immigrant groups within the European economy has a structural importance which makes decisive remediative action difficult to implement. In the past, migrant labour provided a reserve pool of workers, willing to move, work long hours for poor wages and perform the dirty jobs without which our society could not and cannot survive. These jobs lead to little economic or political power and it does not appear to be in the interests of those with power and status that this state of affairs be changed. In other words, the issue of continued inequality in our society has to be squarely addressed. It is within this context that the issue of racism in schools has to be perceived.

Racism in Schools

If British society and its institutions are seen as racist it should be a matter of no surprise that education is seen by many people from racial minorities as doing little for their children in particular, and little for all children, in giving them the help they need to counter this racism. Although black pupils have always been in our state schools it has only been generally perceived in the period since the war, following the increased immigration into the United Kingdom of people from the Caribbean and the Indian sub-continent.

The history of the education system's response makes for sorry reading (e.g. Street-Porter, 1978, Townsend and Brittan, 1972). Fears of schools being swamped, of being turned into 'immigrant schools', are scattered through the literature and policy documents of the period. Teaching in a racially diverse school was seen as a problem, but a problem for the racial minorities to solve. Just as general social policy advocated a view of diversity based on assimilation, so did the schools. Black children were encouraged to adopt and conform to a rather woolly conceptualisation called 'British culture'. If their home language was not English it should be extinguished at school. Their dietary habits, customs and religious beliefs were at best ignored, for such diversity was seen as disturbing and harmful to their development as British citizens.

As policy slowly changed, from assimilation to integration and from integration to cultural pluralism, there was little real change in many of the schools (cf. Street-Porter, 1978, pp. 74–83). All such policy shifts, in practice if not in theory, appeared to many of the minority communities as merely shifts in emphasis. The given power relationships in society were not really questioned and these power relationships in practice ensured the continuation of the exploitation of black people (cf. Mullard, 1980).

That is not to say that cultural pluralism has to be merely a glossy updating of assimilation. It need not be. It encompasses a broad catholicity of practice. At its most effective, it acknowledges the diversity of British society and the unequal power relations with it. It aims, without distorting conventional views of the aims of education, to produce children who can criticall, engage with the issues of diversity and racial oppression. Its focus is not on minority children alone, but is also on the white majority, who, without an appropriate education, will continue to perpetuate racism within society.

Within this broad framework, work has to be done to ensure that the academic achievement of black children is raised from its present disturbingly low levels and that they are not placed in disproportionate numbers in special schools and disruptive units. These are difficult tasks in themselves but are not enough, just as ensuring that equal numbers of boys and girls gain O-level passes in physics is not enough to end discrimination based on gender. Anti-racist, and anti-sexist education has to attempt more. It has to give children the ability to ask difficult and hard-to-answer questions about the society they live in and equip them with the necessary skills and information to start to pose solutions to these questions.

This in turn has implications for the teaching profession and the institutions of schooling generally. Teachers have not been adequately prepared for these challenges; some, if not many, do not in fact wish to take up these challenges. The DES has been slow to give a lead, as have many local authorities. The teacher training and in-service education institutions have also been dilatory. But determined work by committed teachers and others, combined with increasing pressure from minority groups who have seen their children's life chances spoiled by an inadequate education, has had some effect.

An example of this new determination is to be seen in the latest policy proposals put forward by the ILEA (1983a,b,c,d,e and f). These documents, produced after extensive consultation with the black community, face the issue of racism in schools head on. After an analysis of the position and purpose of racism in society they are requesting, in the strongest possible terms, that all educational institutions within the ILEA produce an anti-racist statement. All such statements should contain certain common elements, which they list as:

(i) A clear, unambiguous statement of opposition to any form of racism or racist behaviour.

   (ii) A firm expression of all pupils' or students' rights to the best possible education.

  (iii) A clear indication of what is not acceptable and the procedures, including sanctions, to deal with any transgressions.

  (iv) An explanation of the way in which the school or college intends to develop practices which both tackle racism and create educational opportunities which make for a cohesive society and a local school or college community in which diversity can flourish.

   (v) An outline of the measures by which development will be monitored and evaluated (ILEA, 1983b, p. 25).

At other points in the documents, the specific policies that come from these more broad objectives are spelt out, for example, the forms of sanction that may be taken under element 3, or the ways in which the progress of the policy will be monitored and evaluated. What is interesting about this policy is that it is much more prescriptive and directive than many earlier policy statements in this area, including earlier statements of the ILEA. The question is how far can a central body like the ILEA impose its will on schools and on other educational institutions which by tradition, if not by law, maintain a high level of autonomy, particularly in crucial areas like the curriculum.

However, unless policies like the ILEA's and the black voices which have informed the formulation of such policies are accepted as a valid course for action, it is likely that racism within British society and education will continue to flourish, to the ultimate detriment of all who work and study within it.

NOTES

1   I am grateful to Angela Grunsell for giving me a copy of this poem, 'Babes of the Empire A–Z' by Thomas Stevens, published in 1902.

3 Black Perspectives on British Education

Peter Fraser

The growing body of research on the education of people whose parents or who themselves came from Africa, the Caribbean, or the Indian sub-continent must be treated with great caution. To the problems affecting any study of education are added a number specific to the study of these groups. Most striking is the dispute over the meaning of 'black'. When in the 1960s the researchers were grouping together people from diverse origins, the people themselves were asserting their distinctiveness; when in the late 1970s and the early 1980s researchers recognised the differences, many of the younger people, increasingly native born, had moved towards a more inclusive definition; now that some academics are catching up with that, various cultural-nationalist trends may lead to the construction of new differentiations. The title of this piece uses 'black' in its inclusive sense.

It is difficult for any one person to make sense of the responses to the British education system of all those people grouped together under the name 'black'. What this piece tries to do is to indicate the diversity of black people, various traditional responses to education, what seem to be the major responses and common objections to racist practices.

Finally it is suggested that 'culturalism' can be as bad as racism, and that studies advising teachers to work for the destruction of capitalism to ensure the collapse of racism are of very little help to teachers. (For a thorough survey of the literature see Tomlinson, 1983.)

The Black British

It is useful to remember that there are a number of Black British communities whose residence in Britain long pre-dates 1945.

The great majority, however, arrived in the post-1948 period. By 1981 the effect of various immigration laws was that more than 40 per cent of the Black British were native born. The largest immigrant groups came from the Commonwealth Caribbean, the Indian sub-continent and East Africa. Many were citizens of Britain although their rights as citizens were considerably diminished by immigration and nationality legislation which penalised non-patrials.

From the Commonwealth Caribbean came people who were mainly Christians with similar cultural backgrounds. The migrations from the Indian sub-continent and East Africa were more complex. Religion and cultural practices were closely linked and these varied widely. From India came Sikhs from the Punjab and Hindus from Gujerat; from Pakistan came Muslims from Mirpur and Azad Kashmir; from Bangladesh, Muslims from Sylhet; from East Africa, mainly Kenya and Uganda, came Sikhs, Hindus, Jains and Muslims, part of earlier migrations originating in the Punjab and Gujerat. People who came from the sub-continent were of mainly rural backgrounds, those from East Africa mainly urban, while those from the Caribbean were a mixture with rural backgrounds predominating. Different patterns of family migration also existed, East Africans being the victims of large-scale expulsions arrived as families in the late 1960s and 1970s. Caribbean families had been re-formed from the 1950s onwards but not until the 1960s and 1970s were families from the sub-continent generally reunited. These different cultural and migratory patterns had implications for the school system, i.e. children from different backgrounds might appear in school at the same time and be classified in ways which neglected important distinctions.

There were two major differences between West Indians and those groups loosely called Asians. The latter spoke a variety of languages (Punjabi, Gujerati, Sylheti, Bengali, Hindi, Urdu and Kutchi) while the West Indians spoke varieties of standard English or French (if they came from St Lucia or Dominica for example) and did not regard Creole as a distinct and respectable language. The former were aware that their cultures, like their languages, were distinct; the latter, being European-influenced for centuries, thought that culturally they belonged to the English-speaking family of cultures (this was true even for Trinidadians and Guyanese of Asian origin). Physically a difference was also visible; people from the Caribbean were mainly of African origin. For some time, given different British attitudes to Asians and Africans, this meant that the groups were treated differently by the native-born white population. At the present time the major difference appears to exist between immigrant parents and native-born or native-educated children but this may rapidly disappear since earlier attitudes of accommodation are changing to greater resistance to racist practices.

West Indians and Education in Britain

The major problem with any discussion of West Indian attitudes to education in Britain can be summed up in Taylor's words: 'Somewhat surprisingly, there appears to have been rather little research undertaken explicitly on West Indian pupils' attitudes to school' (Taylor, 1981, p. 175). Much attention has been focused on the underachievement of West Indian pupils but little attention has been given to the views of the underachievers.

Both the Rampton Report (DES, 1981a) and the Scarman Inquiry (Home Office, 1981) identified racist practices as the major concern of the parents. Scarman listed the main objections to schools 'chiefly voiced by West Indian parents' as (i) a lack of discipline in schools; (ii) the stereotyping of West Indians by teachers and their consequent failure to motivate West Indian pupils; (iii) lack of enough contact between parents and schools; (iv) lack of understanding by teachers of their pupils' cultural background; and (v) failure to recognise the distinctive cultural traditions of 'ethnic minorities' in the curriculum. He thought that the lack of contact was the fault of the parents 'who are often, for whatever reason, apparently hesitant to take a full and active part in the schools' (Home Office, 1981, 6.17, 6.22). This statement provides a good enough starting point for a discussion of West Indian attitudes to education.

At a discussion of the Scarman Report in February 1982 at the London University Institute of Commonwealth Studies, Dr Malcolm Cross singled out this particular statement for criticism. He stated that current research in the West Midlands had shown that, on a large number of indicators of parental involvement in schools, West Indian parents had been shown to display greater interest and involvement in their children's schools and schooling than white British or Asian parents. Indeed, Cross commented that anyone knowing the West Indies and the enormous interest there in education would have been surprised with any other result.

Ever since emancipation in 1834, education in the West Indies had been one certain way of upward mobility. Many of the prominent nationalist politicians from the 1930s onwards were the children or grandchildren of teachers or had managed to win scholarships to foreign universities. One of the great attractions of the USA to West Indian migrants throughout the twentieth century was the relative ease, compared to Britain, with which a higher education could be obtained. Many who failed to win scholarships and were disinclined to study law in Britain moved to the USA to obtain university degrees. In the post-Second World War period, the great West Indian migration to Britain was influenced by recruiting agencies and economic opportunities but another influence was the possibility of the migrants' children obtaining secondary and perhaps tertiary education in Britain. At that time in the West Indies secondary schooling had not yet expanded rapidly and university education was also only available to a few. An interest, indeed a belief, in education can therefore be seen as part of the West Indian decision to migrate. Where better to have one's child educated than in Britain with its superior system of education? (Williams, 1951; Figueroa, 1971).

This belief in education had deep cultural roots. The word, the teacher, the educated person were all powerful cultural symbols. The roots, as with so much in the Caribbean, are transoceanic. An important influence is the African respect for the spoken word as carrier of a people's history; the merging of African and European religious traditions; the influential role of Christian ministers in education in the West Indies to this day; the recognition by slaves and ex-slaves of the importance of education was a powerful support to the hegemony of whites in the Caribbean. Foner notes that education was a cultural focus in Jamaica; this finding can be generalised throughout the Caribbean. Foner also observes that while education was no longer the cultural focus for Jamaicans in Britain, they were more involved in their children's education than the native English. She explains that diminished attention to education by pointing out that educational opportunities for these rural Jamaicans were much greater when they moved to Britain: the increasing supply of the commodity had made the demand for it less obsessive but not peripheral (Foner, 1979, pp. 214–16). Another aspect of the West Indian background should be noted. Most adult West Indians came to Britain before any of the territories achieved independence in 1962. Until 1962 the British West Indies had been a place where locally born people, especially those whose skins were dark, had not been able, on the whole, to achieve positions of prominence. Equality of opportunity was thus one of the chief values of these migrating West Indians. This was coupled with a belief that the metropolitan British believed in fair play much more than those found in the colonies. One consequence of this desire for equality of opportunity has been noted by Eric Williams: the attempted introduction of agricultural education in the British West Indies was never very successful since parents regarded it as an inferior form of education which was not given to the fair-skinned potential élite but reserved for the black masses. In England this would appear as resentment of attempts to fob off West Indians with inferior forms of education. (For detailed studies of education in the West Indies, see Figueroa and Persaud, 1976.)

To many, Rastafarianism appears a strange and deviant aspect of West Indian life in Britain. (For popular views, see Kerridge, 1983.) The statement above on the British culture of West Indian immigrants contains a great deal of truth but conceals a great deal also. It leads to a misunderstanding of the current interest in Rastafarianism among young blacks, since some see it merely as the result of rejection by British society, without deep roots in West Indian history. It is true that many West Indians aspired to a level of English culture. Their schooling with its emphasis on the superiority of Britain and the English language and institutions was a powerful agent in inculcating this aspiration. But this schooling never totally neglected the Caribbean, as some of its critics maintain, and it can be argued that the racist beliefs and practices embodied in education prevented many from uncritically accepting this superiority. Even in the nineteenth century there were educated black opponents of racist dismissals of the West Indies like Froude's (Thomas, 1889); even before that time (the late nineteenth century) the historical record shows not insignificant interest and connections with Africa and Black Americans. That interest was maintained in the twentieth century and increased greatly with the Italian invasion of Ethiopia in the 1930s.

Recent research in Jamaica and other Caribbean territories has shown the extent to which a knowledge of Africa, even though mythical, remains a part of the rural West Indian consciousness. In the twentieth century there have been three great expressions of this link with the African continent. The first was Garveyism which had its main focus of activity in the USA but was led by a Jamaican, Marcus Garvey, and had a powerful influence outside the USA. The emphasis of Garveyism was on the political organisation of people of African descent outside Africa; the Pan-African movement stressed the organisation of Africans in Africa to achieve independence. West Indians, for example Henry Sylvester Williams, George Padmore, Ras Makonnan, and C. L. R. James, were prominent in the intellectual leadership (Geiss, 1974). They had been further stimulated by the invasion of Ethiopia which also acted powerfully on the development of the Rastafarian religion (Hill, 1981). In recent years, Rastafarianism has won large numbers of converts in the Caribbean (Cashmore, 1979). Emphasis on the distinctiveness of the West Indian cultural traditions is no mere defensive reaction to events in Britain. Many things which appear new among the Black British of Caribbean origin have their parallels in the lives of their parents. For this reason Foner can conclude that 'by and large despite the bases for cleavage between young and old Jamaicans [i.e. between Jamaicans and their British children], age-related differences do not become the basis for sharp and bitter struggles between them' (Foner, 1979). Rastafarians are part of a long West Indian tradition, not aberrant West Indians. Attitudes to education, therefore, should not be deduced from adherence to Rastafarianism.

West Indians might be termed bi-cultural, i.e. influenced by Europe and Africa; some West Indians are in addition influenced by Asian culture, especially those from Guyana and Trinidad.

The Scarman Report raises another issue, important to West Indian parents, that of discipline. Scarman writes that the objection to a lack of discipline in schools 'partly reflects the different school experience of many West Indian parents, but also other cultural differences'. Leaving aside cultural speculations, it is true that West Indian schools had large rooms with many classes with high pupil/teacher ratios; silence in all classes was a necessity for any teaching to be conducted. Secondary schools could usually afford more relaxed methods of keeping order. From the parents' perspective, education was almost the only hope of their children's success; school was a deadly serious place where the rules had to be followed. So far, then, culture, experience and expectation conspired to insist on over-disciplined behaviour in West Indian schools (Braithwaite, 1952 for attitudes to authority) and the more relaxed methods of

British schools came as a surprise and disappointment to West Indians. But that is not the whole story. There is increasing concern not simply among parents but among pupils at the breakdown in discipline in some London schools which makes life difficult for those still wanting to learn what the school has to teach (London Weekend Television, 1982). There does seem to be a real problem here, not a problem created by West Indian parents with their peculiar experience and culture, as Scarman suggests. A notable feature in recent years is the number of middle-class West Indian parents (very often teachers in the state system) who are sending their children to private schools precisely because of this breakdown in discipline. West Indian parents may tolerate less disorder than other parents but it cannot be denied that there is unacceptable disorder in schools in many areas where the poor and migrants live (Home Office, 1981, 6.17).

Lack of contact between parents and school can be treated fairly briefly. We have already noted that the evidence, despite Scarman, does not suggest that West Indian parents are prone to neglect contacts with schools. What we may have here is a typical case of a group of lay persons (the parents) trying to interact with a group of professionals (the teachers) who, like any professional group, treat lay persons with an amused and condescending attitude and seek to delimit the areas of contact to issues which will not harm the prestige of the professionals, i.e. parents are useful for fund-raising and can be reassured of their children's progress or blamed for their failure, but should not be critical of the performance of the teachers or the content of education. In this case we have a fairly general social process which applies to all parents; West Indian parents may be seen as possessing even less legitimacy than other parents because of the type of criticisms they make. These criticisms query the very basis of the profession's self-image as disinterested agents of the children's improvement.

The Rampton Report noted that the cause of West Indian underachievement 'most forcefully and frequently put forward by West Indians themselves was racism, both within schools and in society'. Many practices can have racist effects, even if they are not motivated by racist beliefs. One such is the tendency of some teachers to stereotype children in what they imagine to be a favourable fashion. Kapo (1981, p. 79), who had all the supposed benefits of an education in Britain, refers forcefully to 'the perpetuation, by white teachers, of the fallacies and myths

about blacks being good at sport and music. Therefore, black
pupils are encouraged at sport and not at academic subjects.
There is a profound inability within the school system to
promote and encourage black pupils to stay on and achieve.'
There are, of course, some who have succeeded in sports and
some who have succeeded in the popular music field. A recent
study by Carrington (1983) notes the illusory promises for so
many of success in sports. He remarks that the overrepresen-
tation, resulting from stereotyping, of West Indians in school
sports teams has 'inadvertently reinforced West Indian academic failure'. Unfavourable stereotypes have had much the
same effect. The Rampton Report said 'there seemed to be a
fairly widespread opinion among teachers to whom we spoke
that West Indian pupils *inevitably* [my emphasis] caused
difficulties'. The report continued 'such negative and patronising attitudes . . . cannot lead to a constructive or balanced
approach to their education'. Low expectations of academic
ability sometimes operate as self-fulfilling prophecies.

Another aspect of this has been the readiness with which
black children of West Indian parents have been labelled as
ESN. It was around this issue that black parents first began to
mobilise, especially as Haringey in London was planning a
system of 'banding' (streaming into ability groupings and
dispersing black children together into the lower ability classes
of schools). Again, we can see here the confluence of the West
Indian experience and British reality. We have already mentioned the sensitivity of West Indians to labels suggesting
inferiority and to types of education rightly seen as meant to
reinforce that inferiority; even in the West Indies the attitudes
of teachers were regarded as important and similar stereotyping
would be resented and resisted. Taylor (1981, pp. 193–9)
rightly says, 'it is not possible [from the research done so far] to
consider teacher expectation towards ethnic minority pupils in
general' and points out that what evidence exists suggests that
teachers 'have generalised views', mainly unfavourable, about
West Indian children. Once more West Indian sensitivity
appears related to the real world.

Less specifically attached to attitudes to West Indians are the
lack of understanding by teachers of the pupils' cultures and the
failure of the curriculum to recognise the value of those cultures.
They can be taken together for a number of reasons: teachers
who had no opportunity to appreciate other cultures can hardly
be expected to understand different cultures; in Britain (and

elsewhere) working-class culture, i.e. the culture of the majority, is neglected in favour of a version of middle-class culture that serves the interest of the élite. What I have called the bi-culturalism of West Indians finds it difficult to survive in Britain. In the West Indies the same teacher who in schools taught the official culture, might well be an important figure in maintaining the submerged tradition. With so few black teachers in the British system one or the other aspect becomes dominant. This may well explain the emphasis West Indian parents place on traditional subjects and their dislike of multicultural education and black studies within the school system (Stone, 1981). They also fear that these innovations may, if confined to the schools which their children attend, serve only to disadvantage them further. This is a failure to understand that multicultural education is not the equivalent of 'Black Studies' in the USA, primarily directed at Black Americans, but education for everyone in a multicultural society. But the opposition can be overstated (Jamdaigni et al., 1982).

One of the earliest studies by Hill (1970) suggested that West Indian boys and girls valued school more than English boys and girls; though the study does not tell us where they were born or how long they lived in Britain, its results seem unexceptionable for the late 1960s. The summary of research presented by Taylor shows that though West Indian or Black British children (distinctions of birth place are rare in the literature) may express negative attitudes to school, they regard education highly, stay on at school longer and often take exams after they have left school. Fuller (1983) makes the same point about the girls: they may be critical of school but they also regard the obtaining of qualifications as very important. The success of the Notting Dale Technology Project in converting 'failures' into competent computer specialists illustrates the success of education outside of school. Why this should be so is illuminated by many recent studies.

Cottle (1978) reveals that many youngsters find teachers refusing to treat them in the same way as other pupils, often neither encouraging nor criticising their black pupils. Jamdaigni (1982, p. 7) provides interviews which confirm these impressions, as does the Afro-Caribbean Educational Resource project (ACER, 1982) document. Some pupils are not, therefore, encouraged to do well since school becomes a place where they are badly treated. Dhondy (1982) offers another range of responses: the pupils who consciously reject school because they realise its futility. What is the point of working hard, acquiring qualifications, if these cannot be translated into jobs? A Black American academic stresses the class nature of British education, noting the greater opportunities available to black Americans and concludes, 'No matter how bright they were, or how much potential they had, black students, living in integrated disadvantaged communities with the lower-class, white indigenous population, would probably wind up not much different from their white working-class counterparts . . .' (Giles, 1977, p. 158). This perception may lead many good pupils to cease bothering in their last years at school. Stone (1981, p. 246) summarises well the most common West Indian judgement of British schools:

> As far as most West Indian parents and children were concerned, the schools do not even begin to offer anything like equal opportunity; they suffer all the disadvantages of the urban-working-class and the additional ones of prejudice and racism . . . it is widely believed . . . that all the most successful West Indians in this country were educated in the Caribbean, at least for most of their school life.

Asians and Education in Britain

Asians and education in Britain are considered to be less of a problem than West Indians and education. This is reflected in the lack of research done on Asian responses to the education system. There are four main reasons for this. In the first place Asians are seen, although increasingly less so, as an undifferentiated mass. The other three reasons flow from this. Asians, it is stated, do as well or better at school than the white English. Underachievement is not seen as a problem. This, however, masks great differences: some Asians do very well, many do very badly. This is not unconnected with the diverse streams of immigration. Many of the immigrants from East Africa were professional people, others were successful businessmen. The children of poor rural Bangladeshis who now work in menial, poorly-paid, and exhausting jobs and live in poor housing, do very badly. The global statistics tend to gloss over these differences. Thirdly, the stereotype of the Asian as docile and hard-working, contrasts markedly with the contradictory West Indian stereotype of being simultaneously lazy, passive and withdrawn and boisterous, aggressive and disruptive. The stereotypes held by teachers of Asians may not have been a barrier to their education but we should not be too sanguine. Lastly, and more controversially, the recognition that Asians needed to learn English meant that extra attention was paid to their special needs. We will come back to this. A similar recognition that West Indians might need help was absent and has now surfaced when most of the children have been born and brought up here.

Having a distinct culture was probably an advantage to Asian immigrants. This provided some insulation from the anti-intellectualism of British culture, at least for the children born outside Britain. It also meant for the children that what was offered in schools was new and different from what the community offered – the difficulties of coping with what was offered could not be minimised.

Significant, too, was the importance attached to learning in the cultures of the Asian immigrants. Hinduism, Islam and Sikhism all attach importance to the written word. For some parents, even some from impoverished rural backgrounds, their religion would thus have placed a high value on education. Different cultural practice and language coupled with discriminatory practices in society at large tended to keep some children isolated from those elements of working-class English culture antagonistic to education and made them aware of the problems of acquiring English culture.

All has not been plain sailing, however. The perception of Asians as a problem in the schools began to appear in the early 1960s. White parents in places of high immigrant concentration began to complain that the schools attended by their own children were being 'swamped by Asians'. In 1963 the Secretary of State for Education decided that 33 per cent was the maximum permissible percentage of immigrant children in any one school. Thus began the policy of bussing – the similarity with the banding in Haringey should be noted. There was little opposition at first from Asian parents – bussing was not immediately associated with categorising Asian children as inferior.

Black parents, by and large, initially approved of bussing. Keen to secure the best possible education for their children, they thought dispersal would mean smaller classes, more individual attention and, above all, integration into the English school system for their children. They were soon to be disillusioned (Campaign against Racism and Fascism (CARF)/Southall, 1981, pp. 31–5).

Why was this? In the first place bussing in a place like Southall was along a one-way street. Asians were bussed out, whites were never bussed in. This enabled the council to refuse to build new schools in Southall although the school-age population was growing. Children had to be moved to schools outside the area, it was argued, therefore there was no necessity for new schools in Southall itself.

In the second place, all Asian children were assessed and automatically put into reception classes even when their first language was English (we have noted above the complexity of 'Asian' migration; many East African Asians spoke English). Reception classes were physically separated from the rest of the school and often the only educational interaction was with the remedial classes. Classes were frequently quite large and transferring from them to normal classes took a long time and often resulted in transfer to lower streams of the school. Thus dispersal might well mean larger classes, less individual attention and segregation from the rest of the school. Teachers working in such schools described them as 'divided into three social groups, which didn't mix: English children, Indian children in the main school, and reception class children. In the frequent racial fights, reception class children are usually the targets' (CARF/Southall, 1981).

Bussing also had another side effect. Asian children were often attacked while waiting for the buses to arrive: teachers at some schools had to guard the children; at others the children formed their own protective groups; children were sent home early from some schools thereby missing five lessons a week; and in 1975 a fifteen-year-old boy was killed during an inter-school fight (CARF/Southall, 1981, p. 47). The issues arising from bussing forced parents to take action. Representations eventually led to a Race Relations Board investigation of bussing which concluded that it 'may be discriminatory for those who have no educational need for it'. Three years later, in 1978, Ealing Council threatened with prosecution by various black organisations finally agreed to build two new schools in Southall.

Parents were not only concerned with bussing, however. They questioned the frequency with which their children were suspended, the prejudiced attitudes of teachers and the persistence of racially motivated attacks on their children within the schools. Other matters, apparently minor to some head teachers, like forcing Muslim girls to wear skirts, were also issues which parents saw as evidence of cultural domination within the British education system.

Even where the school system had seemed to be sensitive and responsive to the needs of Asian children, the provision of language teaching had been counter-productive. The failure to recognise that some Asian children were fluent in English was mentioned above. Alladina (1983, pp. 12–19) has noted that for many who were not speakers of English these special classes were unsatisfactory introductions to the school system, differing from ordinary classes in standards of classroom behaviour, discipline and curriculum. There was a lack of adequate teaching material and some teachers 'speak to these children in an idiosyncratic variety of "pidgin" English all in the name of language teaching'. He does mention that there have been some developments, especially the idea of collaborative teaching, using mainstream classes and close support from mother-tongue teaching in the same schools. One of the consequences of the failure of previous programmes is the 'many children in ESL classes who do not have competence in English but are also not literate in their home language and lack more advanced concepts in their language'. These effects and the close connection between language and culture have coloured the responses of many parents.

Some parents have responded by seeking their own means of preserving their culture. This can take the form of setting up supplementary schools, which has also been attempted by the West Indian community (and has been done by post-war Polish immigrants to Britain). These schools are undoubtedly useful in preserving and transmitting cultural traditions; Anwar, noting the worries expressed by Pakistani parents about the behaviour of English children and its possible deleterious effect on their children, writes of 'the importance attached to the transmission of religion and culture to Pakistani children who were born and brought up in England. This was mentioned [by their parents] in almost every context' (Anwar, 1979, p. 216).

The extreme form of this is to attempt to set up religious schools, for example for Sikhs, a suggestion to which the more radical, such as Dheer, are totally opposed. Nagra (1981/2, pp. 431–6) points out the difficulties that the supplementary schools face in his study of those in Coventry: poor financing and extra burdens on the children and the difficulty with limited resources: of successfully implementing their aims which are (i) to enable children to communicate with parents and other persons of their own community (language); (ii) to give children a sense of identity (culture); (iii) to assist them to understand and participate more fully in particular socio-cultural contexts (socialisation); and (iv) to pass on religion and culture. Their task in sum is, as Dheer puts it for multicultural education in the official system, to challenge the 'biased British/European world view reinforced by the system of education over centuries'. But they do this by concentrating on the minority communities and with only limited resources (Dheer, 1982).

What about the consumers of the official system – the youngsters themselves? Although their performance is better than that of West Indian children, it is interesting to see how alike the criticisms are. Wilson cites many examples of racist attitudes and remarks from primary school teachers in Southall. She describes the generally ethno-centric attitudes among the educators and continues:

> Children between eight and twelve seem too young to fight against cultural racism in school; it is as though they are almost stunned into accepting the inferiority with which white society has labelled them. But at twelve their feelings seem to change. It is not that racism vanishes – in fact it intensifies and violence increases, but most children start to face up to it at this point, and their 'inferiority' usually clears away . . . Previously their view of Britain was conditioned by their parents' expectations. Now they can reject these and look back more objectively at the implicitly racist atmosphere of their primary school days.

It should also be noted that their parents have become much more militant in recent years and the magnificent struggle of Asian women for rights at work, often against official union apathy and opposition, has been one of the major influences in the Asian community losing its docile stereotype. A young schoolboy illustrates exactly the transition of which Wilson writes:

> I remember thinking when I was younger that maybe, somehow, my language – the language of my parents – isn't a real language . . . All our history is from a British point of view. We're taught that Robert Clive was a hero and how the British introduced the railway and democracy to India . . . but we're never told how Indian industry was smashed by and replaced by British industry . . . what we are saying all the time is that white is right. So we grow up with English nicknames and no self-respect.

From this last quotation we can see that the official system not only fails to prepare children to pass examinations but fails to maintain the dominance of the élite ideology – that young man has plainly *not* lost his self-respect or accepted the white version of history (Wilson, pp. 87–102; CARF/Southall, p. 46).

The reasons for this are clear. Wilson notes that 'when racism takes the form of violence, they can't fail to recognise it as an attack on themselves, and part of a value system they cannot go along with'. Asian boys and girls seem to be the targets of violence of a racial nature in school far more than West Indians – indeed, at times West Indians have been the attackers. (There is evidence that the growth of what Barker calls the new racism may well be forcing West Indians and Asians to admit their common problems and may be eliminating this type of attack.) The girls that Wilson interviewed all noted the frequent racial fights and a former pupil (male) of an Ealing school said, 'There were racial fights every day – even going through the corridors you were in danger of attack. The teachers would lock their rooms and just carry on teaching. Outside the school the violence would continue and people would come out of their houses to support white kids.' Again, outside the school parents are themselves subject to a high probability of assault, with the police this time in the position of those who are just not interested – the experience of parents and children have become very similar.

Asian girls have proved a particularly difficult problem for the school system. Attitudes to female education vary quite widely among the Asian community and are dependent on religion, class, area of migration, whether urban or rural. Urban Hindus or East African Asians are likely to have quite 'progressive' attitudes to their daughters' education and be willing for them to receive a university-level education. Muslim parents from peasant backgrounds might consider their daughters' education an irrelevance. But for all types of Muslim parents, from peasants to urban sophisticates, religious dictates conflict with the shibboleths of the British education system. Muslim women must cover their arms and legs; the British school system thinks women in trousers – whether pupils or teachers – unseemly; the conflict is irreconcilable. There have been examples in places like London and Bradford of the complete insensitivity of headteachers and educational authorities to this and the coercion of Muslim girls into wearing skirts or shorts for physical education. There are similarities here with the opposition to the turban and other items of male Sikh dress. This insensitivity causes great distress to the families concerned and when it reaches the newspapers is presented as further evidence of Asian intransigence and cultural separatism. The assumption behind this seems to be that the dominant culture is wholly superior, that of minorities wholly inferior. Asian girls are hence probably the most stressed group among the children of ethnic minorities. Their position may well improve with the growing militancy of Asian women workers.

To summarise the Asian experience of the British school system – Asians leave school with better qualifications than West Indians but suffer enormously in the schools themselves from racism and violence and the girls suffer, in addition, from the cultural arrogance of those in authority who are unwilling to accept different practices. The picture painted by the examination results may only serve to augment the complacency of those who wish to deny the existence of racism in British schools.

Supplementary Schools, Separate Schools?

A common reaction by both West Indians and Asians has been to set up supplementary schools or to contemplate separate schools. These moves can proceed from diverse considerations. Supplementary schools may be set up to make good the perceived deficiencies of education provided normally. We have seen that there is much evidence to suggest the truth of this perception. Supplementary schools may have more cultural focuses, i.e. there exists dissatisfaction not with what is provided normally but with the omissions of the normal system. These deficiencies may relate to the history, culture and language of the group establishing such a school. If there is dissatisfaction with the normal offering, whether this be the result of the alleged incompatibility of the group's culture with that taught in the school or a more specific objection to mixed sex schools, there arises the demand for separate schools. In this section we shall see that there are many common themes in the West Indian and Asian calls for supplementary or separate schools.

Until very recently, among West Indians there was not felt to be cultural incompatibility between the school and the pupils. Now however there is the strong feeling that schools have failed children of West Indian background, thus supplementary schools tend to replicate ordinary schools. Approaches to teaching are inclined to be orthodox, even old-fashioned, and the subjects are the same as in ordinary schools. In some, African and Caribbean literature is taught but the strong impression is of an attempt to redress disadvantage within the terms established by the state system. Among Bangladeshis, the most disadvantaged of all the groups discussed in this chapter, there are similar attempts to use supplementary schools in this way. Since supplementary schools are so small, poorly financed and little known, it is difficult to produce figures, but much less than 10 per cent of the West Indian or Asian population use them. They nevertheless indicate the willingness of parents in difficult circumstances to improve the education of their children (Stone, op. cit.).

Supplementary schools which have as their object the transmission of cultural knowledge and language may express dissatisfaction with what schools offer rather than their failures. They may be an acknowledgment that the school system cannot cope adequately with more than one culture at a time and that parents must play a role. Those West Indian supplementary schools which emphasise African or Caribbean history and literature are edging towards such a position. Some clearly embody a demand for the widening of the curriculum; others are more clearly like Polish or Jewish supplementary schools in that they are designed to add another cultural resource to their children who may perform well in ordinary schools. This is the case with a number of Asian supplementary schools. Some are language schools to ensure that the children, who are taught and learn in English, do not forget their parents' language or become cut off from the literature and written cultural heritage of their parents.

These schools may have important effects on the performance of children in ordinary schools. The smaller classes and expert tuition (for many are run by trained teachers), especially by people without preconceptions of low ability and culturally or racially determined capabilities, might well motivate pupils and prepare them better for their schools. They may, therefore, as some have done in the past, challenge teachers' notions about the ability of pupils who are poorly esteemed. Those that concentrate on cultural or linguistic training can contribute to the education not only of the pupils who attend them but also of other pupils and teachers, and help to destroy some of the parochialism so prevalent in the education system.

Parochialism, however, is not the prerogative of the British education system or society alone. The recent vigour of fundamentalist religions of all types has important implications for attitudes to the school system. The vigour of fundamentalism, both within nations and internationally, has much to do with groups feeling threatened by the cultural arrogance of powerful political forces, whether super-power or dominant cultural groups. These fundamentalist religious tendencies are often allied with tendencies towards cultural-nationalism. While the frequency of racist practices is often given as a reason for separate schools, the religious and cultural/national tendencies also fuel this movement. Some West Indians have argued that separate schools alone can protect children from racism in all its forms, and give them pride and self-confidence. Interestingly enough, the school usually cited as proof that separate West Indian schools can work, since it has almost all black staff and pupils, belongs to a fundamentalist Christian denomination. The case is clearer when we look at the call for separate Muslim schools.

Much of the appeal of separate schools for Muslim communities has been created by the decline in the provision of single-sex schools. There may be excellent social and educational reasons for co-educational schools; these are unlikely to appeal to any group of people who believe that girls and boys should be educated differently, or at the very least educated similarly but separately. The concern for the continuation of separate but not different schools is not confined to Muslims. With strict or fundamentalist Muslims, however, the difference between men and women is regarded as such an important part of their religious beliefs and practices that it fuels the call for separate schools.

The main thrust for separate schools may be seen as an extension of the concern about the preservation of cultures which, as we have seen, may simply take the form of supplementary schools. When parents become worried that their children are becoming too Westernised and feel that Westernisation and their culture are incompatible, supplementary schools will not be enough. In the eyes of such parents, what the ordinary school provides can only be of little importance compared to education in the principles of their culture. This seems to be the position of a growing minority of strict Muslim parents. As a religious body they, of course, have a right to 'voluntary-aided' status so that unlike minorities defined by ethnic origin rather than religious affiliation, there does exist a possibility that such schools will be established. Supporters of separate schools argue that they will contribute more to harmony and a true appreciation of cultural diversity than ordinary schools. In so far as they are the result of the revival of fundamentalist Islam, there is and was little that the British school system could do to satisfy these demands; greater sensitivity to cultural diversity and the sensibilities of parents might have made the ground less fertile for separatist arguments (Anwar, 1983).

Is the Research Useful for Teachers?

Some of the major themes in West Indian and Asian reaction to the British school system have been outlined. The categories 'West Indian' and 'Asian' have been treated in a way that suggests greater homogeneity than actually exists. In attempting to indicate the common objections of each group and the similarities of these objections, it is easy to replace one stereotype by another. Important considerations have been omitted: the difference in class attitudes existing in both groups, differences concerned with the regional origin of people, differences within Britain itself in racial attitudes, the living conditions of and educational provision for immigrant groups. All these have to be taken into account and, in the end, the teacher has to deal in class with an individual child, not with its class origins, or supposed racial or cultural origins.

It is important for the teacher who has avoided the trap of 'racial' categorisation, whether by luck, judgement, or self-education, not to fall into the trap of cultural categorisation. At its crudest, this might mean assuming that any West Indian conforms to some fictional notion of West Indian culture, or that any Asian will conform to an equally fictional notion of Asian culture. It would be a disaster if racial notions were replaced by cultural notions which act in the same way as skin colour or race have acted in the past.

A number of recent studies, linking racism with capitalism, have reduced the role of teachers to mere guardians of the status quo, whether they wish to be so or not, and assert that the real struggle is somewhere else (Mullard, 1983; Centre for Contemporary Cultural Studies (CCCS), 1982). The job of passing on skills and inculcating humane values is difficult enough as it is. Teachers have one of the most difficult jobs and would do well to be wary of any researcher who tells them that nothing good can be done until the millenium dawns.

4 Socialisation in Schools in Multicultural Societies

Eigil Pedersen

> Of all the vulgar modes of escaping from the consideration of the effect of social and normal influences on the human mind, the most vulgar is that of attributing the diversities of conduct and character to inherent natural differences (John Stuart Mill).

The purpose of this chapter is to examine the implications for multicultural education that can be drawn from studies of the socialisation of children in primary school classes in Britain and North America.

A majority of individuals now living in the northern industrialised parts of America (United States and Canada) are descended from Caucasian immigrants who arrived in the past century or so. Most immigrants could be identified as such by language or accent, dress, deportment, or other signs, but their children could easily merge with the larger population, being not visibly different.

North American society was, and remains, highly stratified into socio-economic classes, and with few exceptions, immigrants were recruited into the lowest strata. However, a rapidly-expanding economy made for high rates of upward social mobility, and in many cases, low-status immigrant parents could watch with satisfaction and pride as their American-born children 'moved up in the world'. Education played an important part in this, since, in the United States schooling had as one of its official purposes the 'Americanisation' of 'foreigners'. While upward social mobility was high, many newcomers seemed eager to adopt their new nationality.

However, not all immigrants were Caucasians, nor were all migrants to the industrial North 'foreigners'. The sudden demand for factory workers that arose during the two world wars encouraged internal migration from the relatively rural South to large and growing black urban communities in the North. Similar migrations to Britain occurred following the Second World War with the arrival of visibly different people from the Indian sub-continent, the British West Indies, Africa and other places. Again, most of these immigrants had to start at the bottom of the socio-economic-status ladder, resulting in their concentration in ethnic or racial enclaves or ghettoes in the decaying inner cities. In both North America and Britain, this migration coincided with a levelling-off of industrial development, which, along with the attendant economic crisis, has swelled the ranks of the unemployed. As usual, the least well-established bear the brunt of joblessness. It is again a case of 'last hired, first fired', but, under the circumstances just described, it results in a pattern where people of one colour tend to have access to gainful occupations, while those of another tend to be unemployed. Ghettoes are widely seen to be 'problem' neighbourhoods.

Schools serving visible minorities are also seen by the general public as 'problem' schools. Many people seem to accept the old-fashioned American idea that the function of such schools is to socialise the pupils so that they can be absorbed into the mainstream culture; but can schools carry out their traditional role of 'Americanising' or 'making British' the new arrivals who, because of their skin colour, cannot be expected to merge unnoticed with the rest of the population in a mere generation or two? Besides, do immigrants, visible or not, really want to be 'absorbed'?

It has recently become fashionable to criticise the schools for not producing graduates who are immediately employable; and with the concentration of the 'dangerously idle' in ghettoes, there is a tendency to blame 'problem' schools. However, it seems unrealistic to believe that, at least in the short run, schools can reform the economy and solve the problem of minority unemployment.

What can the schools be expected to achieve in a multicultural society? I believe that they must address themselves to two closely related goals: first, they must equip their students with the knowledge and skills required to make valuable and satisfying contributions to the general common good through gainful employment: second, the whole population must be made aware that equal opportunity of access for *all* members of the multicultural society to a fair share of work that is socially important and personally fulfilling must be available. In short, schools must strive to prepare *all* the children for useful and happy lives, and they must also work to eliminate the prejudice in the larger population that leads to discrimination against minorities. The level of discrimination against members of racial and ethnic minorities – and women – in North America and Britain suggests that the schools serving children of the majority culture are failing as well. In short, multicultural education is the urgent concern of all the schools, not just those 'problem' schools which serve (or disserve) the children of visible and cultural minorities.

Can schools serving minority children become more effective in helping them to achieve their highest potential?

Most adults in modern industrial societies believe that schooling and technical training are becoming increasingly important in preparing the young adult for work-roles, and that, as a general rule, the more complex or responsible the work, the more schooling required, and the larger the financial and social-status rewards. Education is thought to be the key to social mobility after all, since schooling is not only available to all, but is also compulsory and free; everyone has the opportunity to achieve any social status deserved – it is just a matter of taking advantage of what is offered in school and working hard. Those who do not avail themselves of the opportunity have no one to blame but themselves.

Is it true?

There is no doubt that for the vast majority in a modern industrial society, schooling is essential to the achievement of virtually any occupation that offers moderate or higher social status. But many social scientists, for example Coleman *et al.* (1966) and Jencks *et al.* (1972) seem to argue that schooling makes very little difference; even those such as Sewell (1980) and Rutter *et al.* (1979) who take the opposite tack show that mobility is usually very modest.

Social mobility does occur, but it appears that children from ghetto schools are much more likely to keep their low status than to move very far up the ladder. Do teachers play any part, conscious or not, in enhancing or preventing the upward mobility of their pupils? If so, why and how do they do it? Are there any systematic racial, ethnic, gender, or socio-economic biases in their selection of pupils to sponsor or to hinder? Are there any conclusions we could draw from the research that might offer suggestions, however tentative, for making the efforts of teachers more beneficial to all the children?

Six Studies of Early Formal Schooling

Because it seems that the child's early teachers establish patterns that are difficult to change later (for a discussion of some of the reasons underlying this, see Pedersen and Faucher, 1978) this chapter focuses on six studies of early formal schooling that may help to answer the above questions. The studies are by Talcott Parsons (1959), Ray Rist (1970), Eigil Pedersen and T. A. Faucher (1978), Rachel Sharp and Anthony Green (1975), Jean Anyon (1981) and Eigil and Madge Pedersen (1982). Parsons was American, as are Rist and Anyon; Sharp and Green made their observations in England; and the Pedersens and Faucher conducted most of their work in Canada.

Parsons (1959) described the school as an agency not only of socialisation, but of allocation to social ranks as well: 'The primary selective process occurs through differential school performance in elementary school . . . [and] ascriptive (i.e. social class, which is often linked to racial and ethnic membership) as well as achieved factors influence the outcome' (p. 229). Parsons argued that classroom activities are structured as a contest, in which the imposition of a common set of tasks on *ostensibly* equal competitors results in winners and losers. However, since the curriculum assumes knowledge and skills not characteristic of minority children, they are inevitably over-represented among the losers.

The presence of so many losers in society could cause problems, especially if they were bitter and rebellious. But Parsons identifies another function of the contest which is to make the losers feel that they have had a fair chance, that their failure is their own 'fault'. This is reinforced by the teacher's definition of the 'good' pupil. 'A good pupil is defined in terms of the fusion of the cognitive and moral' . . . in other words, the good pupil is not only one who learns well, but who behaves well, too (p. 304). Thus, he introduces the notion that those who do not learn well are considered by others, and consider themselves, in a negative sense, deviant. Of course, when teachers group children, the deviants become highly noticeable, especially if a majority of the losers are recognisable members of minority groups.

Parsons' theoretical work has since been followed by research conducted in classrooms. For example, Rist (1970) observed a single cohort of children for almost three years, through kindergarten, Grade One and into Grade Two. He noted that after only eight days of working with the class as a whole aggregate, the kindergarten teacher, Mrs Caplow, assigned the children to 'ability groups' at three tables. The proportion of children from low-income, large families was higher at the lowest-ability table (Table Three) than at Table One. Also, there seemed to be more children with very dark skin at Table Three, despite the fact that the teacher, herself black, was an active civil rights worker! (One of the effects of racism can be that even the victims of negative stereotypes may behave as if those stereotypes were true.) The 'teams' had been chosen, and the unequal contest, as earlier hypothesised by Parsons, was under way.

At first, only the teacher treated the 'low-ability' pupils as if they were stupid and slow, but after the passage of some days, the children at Table One began imitating her, using childish language ('He don't know – He stupid – It's sixteen, dummy'); and after the passage of weeks, the children at Table Three began insulting one another – never the 'brighter' children – using terms such as 'egg-head', 'nigger', and 'dumb-dumb'. Table Three children had internalised their inferior status. By the end of the year, all Table One children were 'promoted' to Grade One, whereas many Table Two and Table Three pupils had 'failed'. For each child, Mrs Caplow's early judgement had become a self-fulfilling prophecy.

Teachers influence the academic achievement of their children by linking their estimates of the pupils' academic potential to their socio-economic or racial affiliations, and then by offering more effective instruction to those whom they expect to succeed. But does assignment to low-ability groups have lasting impact on subsequent social-status achievement, and is the teacher's influence necessarily negative?

Pedersen and Faucher (1978) reported a study in which the socio-economic status of a sample of young adults who had formerly all been pupils in the same inner-city, elementary 'problem' school was measured. The school's permanent records for these former pupils were examined to determine antecedents of upward social mobility. Three major predictors emerged: the higher the relative socio-economic status of the father, the higher the subsequent socio-economic status of the child: the larger the number of siblings, the smaller the likelihood of achieving relatively high socio-economic status: and (the strongest factor) those who had been exposed to a particular grade one teacher – Miss A – were significantly more likely to have relatively higher socio-economic status in adulthood than those exposed to the other Grade One teachers.

Further analysis of the permanent records revealed that Miss A's former pupils had achieved substantially higher mean academic grades and had received higher teacher-estimates of personal qualities such as effort, leadership and initiative on their report cards in *all* subsequent elementary grades than had the former pupils of other Grade One teachers during the same eleven-year span. It was concluded that Miss A had done a superior job of teaching reading and other subjects, and in addition had treated her pupils in ways that had developed in them good work habits and self-respect.

Apparently, not all teachers have the same effects on children as Mrs Caplow.

Of course, factors other than schooling influence social mobility. Miss A certainly seemed to enhance the later social status of her pupils, and probably achieved this by being a superior teacher of academic subjects who inspired in them good attitudes towards work and towards themselves. There is no evidence that there were any systematic racially-linked differences in the later *academic* achievement of her former pupils, but subsequent stepwise multiple-regression analyses of academic achievement and personal quality variables against adult status as the dependent variable for blacks and whites separately listed academic achievement as the first and by far strongest predictor of adult status for whites, whereas the personal qualities came out first for blacks, with academic achievement at the bottom of the list! This suggests that employers (most of whom were presumably former pupils of middle- and upper-class schools) seek different characteristics in blacks as compared to whites, and supports our contention that it is not just the 'problem' schools that must be reformed.

The studies we have just described briefly examined traditional schools in which children were assigned to their classrooms on the basis of age. Pupils were expected to reach certain standards of achievement, and their teachers (with the possible exception of Miss A) used methods which very soon made it obvious which ones were doing well and which poorly. Following this revelation, some sort of group-membership was usually assigned, resulting in a label being attached to each child.

The findings of many classroom studies suggest that the academic stratification that emerges tends to reflect the stratification of the society in which the schools are embedded. One reason for this reflected stratification (Bourdieu, 1977, calls it reproduction) may be the biased contest that so often seems to take place. If so, we might speculate that were the contestative character of early schooling eliminated, reproduction might not occur.

Sharp and Green (1975) observed classrooms in a 'progressive' English primary school which used a family-grouping system such that there was a broader age-range among pupils in the same classroom than is usual. Each child was expected to learn at an individual speed without receiving formal group or whole-class instruction: therefore, direct comparisons among 'equal' contestants were not possible. In addition, the teachers were aware of the danger of classifying and labelling the children early in their schooling.

Nevertheless, Sharp and Green were forced to conclude that, 'The processes we have observed in the classroom . . . can be seen as the initial stages of the institutionalisation of social selection for the stratification system' (p. 221). Why did well-meaning teachers have effects on the children that they had apparently never intended in the first place?

The authors noted that despite the ideology of individual advancement, nevertheless the school is held accountable to teach literacy and numeracy. Furthermore, whatever the organisation or social structure of the classroom, the need to maintain control tends to give rise to certain patterns of teacher behaviour. Sharp and Green asserted that we cannot understand the social interaction processes unless we take into account the larger social structure of which they are a part, and unless we pay attention to the physical and material context as well. And, despite employing a Marxist sociological viewpoint very different from Parsons' structural-functional model, they came to remarkably similar conclusions. 'As we have observed in the classroom, the social advancement of the few depends upon a denial of the same for the many, as pupils' careers are socially structured through the activities of educators who are themselves enclosed within a wider structure of constraints over which they have little control' (p. 224).

Sharp and Green suggested that the fault lies in the structure of the larger society itself, and concluded that, 'unless or until educators are able to comprehend their own structural location and develop theories of the limits of feasible political action to transform that location, they will continue to be unwilling victims of a structure that undermines the moral concerns they profess' (p. 227).

Apparently, teachers often influence negatively the social mobility of their pupils, not consciously and certainly not willingly, but because the social structure and physical environment impose expectations for, and constraints upon, their actions. Sharp and Green suggested that teachers should understand how the structural location thwarts their good intentions, and that we should study what political actions could be applied in an effort to change this. The implication of their conclusions seems to be that we should not waste time trying to change schooling, but should instead change society.

Sharp and Green present a good case for the necessity to do more than merely try to improve the schools: but their views on schooling seem to me to be unreasonably deterministic. If we believe that the teachers can't help what they do under current social circumstances, then we are not likely to work hard towards the improvement of such things as curriculum and classroom interaction patterns.

Can teacher-pupil interaction patterns be improved? Is there no hope of improving teaching practice, or will it be necessary to wait until society has been reformed? The work of Anyon (1981) suggests a cautiously optimistic answer to this question, and in a similar vein, Giroux (1983) sketches a 'theory of resistance' which offers some suggestions for a new pedagogy.

Anyon made observations in Grade Two and Grade Five classrooms of five different schools, chosen to cover four distinct social class levels: working class, middle class, affluent professional class, and executive élite. Among her important findings were that, although the curriculum is prescribed, there are moderate but important differences in the materials and texts being used at the various class levels, and more important, differences in the way the materials are employed – the 'curriculum-in-use' – and the reactions of pupils to those differences.

Anyon seems to have been influenced by ideas similar to those that led Gouldner (1971), in his discussion of the social system and the self, to write,

The self may . . . exercise self-*esteem* when it *conforms* to the
expectations of others . . . But self-esteem is not the same as self-
regard, which arises from a sense of the self's *potency*. Self-esteem
derives from *consensual* validation: self-regard derives from *con-
flictual* validation, which the self may experience when it manifestly
becomes something to be reckoned with . . . (p. 221).

Perhaps this is why Anyon seems pleased to note that the
children in the two working-class schools do not simply sit back
and accept what is being done to them, but actually resist. The
resistance of the working-class children is one of the observations that provides the basis for Anyon's optimism.

Unfortunately it is difficult to read resistance into her
description of what is actually happening: perhaps her optimism is based more on what she hoped to find than what was
actually taking place. I agree with Hargreaves' (1982) contention that one of the forms of 'resistance' identified by Anyon as
'withholding enthusiasm' may simply be a retreatist response
(on retreatism in students, see Pedersen and Etheridge, 1970)
rather than resistance.

Earlier reports by other Marxist social scientists, for example
Bowles and Gintis (1976), suggested that schools merely
reproduce the social-class stratification arrangements of the
societies in which they exist. Anyon, however, argues that
schools also reproduce the tensions and conflicts of the larger
society, and that such conflicts contain the seeds of transform-
ation. Her hope is that schools can actually help to bring about
social change. In fact, she concludes that, ' . . . perhaps the
most important implication . . . is that for those of us who are
working to transform society, there is much to do, at all levels, in
education' (p. 39). And Giroux (1983) suggests that, 'schools
will not change society, but we can create in them pockets of
resistance that provide pedagogical models for new forms of
learning and social relations – forms which can be used in other
spheres more directly involved in the struggle for a new morality
and view of social justice' (p. 293).

However, one person's hope may be another person's despair.
It seems cruel and highly unfair that the hope of working-class
children for a decent future (and working-class children would
currently include more than a proportional share of minority
children) should be based on their rejection of schooling, which
would require them to oppose the wishes of their parents.
Gundara (1981) has noted that in the early sixties, a first

generation of blacks in Britain had felt that schooling was important: 'In the UK, the black parents noticed that the first generation of black children were not educated to the high standards they had expected of the British education system. This was a terrible blow, because while the parents had settled for lower status jobs, they had expected their children at least to fare better' (p. 4).

Minority children should have the right to decide for themselves whether to be revolutionaries or to adopt a more traditional role of earning a reasonable living in the society in which they live. They deserve not to have to reject the employment opportunities that success in schooling might offer. (Besides, well-educated revolutionaries are probably more effective than ignorant ones!) I believe we must continue to search for more effective means of providing minority children with good, effective education, as well as doing our part as citizens to help change our society. This will, among many other things, involve attempts to discover how effective teachers such as Miss A go about encouraging the better-than-average results their pupils achieve.

A Case Study of Two Classes

It was in quest of this goal that Pedersen and Pedersen (1982) undertook the study of two traditional Grade One classes in multi-ethnic, multi-racial, inner-city schools in a large North American city. Two teachers of contrasting personality, but as alike in other respects as possible, were observed during the first twenty days of the school year, as contrasting social systems unfolded in the two classrooms.

Both teachers, Miss Smith and Miss Jones, were single women with more than twenty years' experience in teaching first grade. They were absolutely devoted to the children, and very serious and conscientious about their work. However, their teaching styles were in striking contrast.

Miss Smith's teaching style had evolved out of the view of other adults, since, reasoning that it was hard enough to meet her responsibilities in such a difficult school without the added distractions of student teachers or other visitors, she had kept other adults out of her class. The school was run on a very traditional pattern. Parents were not welcome to visit the classrooms. Children assembled each morning in the basement and moved to their classes in orderly lines by twos at the sound of the bell. The classroom, too, was regimented, with the seats in straight rows which occupied virtually all of the available floor space. The aim of this seemed to be to keep the children as far from one another as possible, and was undoubtedly intended to enhance the teacher's control, which seemed to be her obsession. In fact, the meek manner of the children's arrival on the very first day of school seemed to indicate that they already knew they were to be very quiet. When they forgot, they were reminded in no uncertain terms, and if they began squirming in their seats, they were required to sit still with their hands folded on top of their heads.

Individuals were frequently given severe 'tongue-lashings' in a public manner which seemed deliberately designed to make others 'sit up and take notice'. Pupils spoke only when given permission by the teacher, and then it was often because they were required to admit some misbehaviour or to confess some personal shortcoming.

Miss Smith seemed to expect trouble, and tried to 'head it off'. Children who made mistakes were made to recite the rules: if they could do so, they were accused of having broken them deliberately: if they could not repeat them, they were blamed for not having paid attention. Either way, they were guilty, and deserving of punishment.

After the routines designed to establish absolute teacher-control had been laid down, Miss Smith then began teaching subject-matter. The first formal lesson was on printing the letter 'l'. This was taught by rules, too. Children who for whatever reason could not immediately print the letter 'l' to the 'mastery' standard of which their teacher was so proud, were asked to recite the rules: 'Start at the top line. Straight down. *Touch* the bottom line.' And so on. There would inevitably be loud queries on the part of the teacher: 'Do you start *above* the line?' Child: 'No.' Teacher: 'No, *who?*' Child: 'No, Miss Smith.' And so on. Such children were treated not as if they were perhaps not yet ready to write, or might need more time to develop the skill, but as if they, having broken the rules, were bad. This recalls the quote from Parsons on page 3: 'a *good* pupil is defined in terms of the cognitive and moral'.

On the afternoon of the fifth day, Miss Smith divided the class into three reading groups, calling their names from lists which she had prepared some time before. These groups were highly correlated with race and ethnicity: English-speaking whites dominated the high group, English-speaking blacks the middle group, and Portuguese-speaking white children (many of whom spoke very little English) the bottom group. Miss Smith then gave formal lessons by groups, always beginning with the high and ending with the low, after she had run out of time and patience. The pupils in Group One were seated near her desk, whereas the children in Group Three sat on the opposite side of the classroom from the teacher. Pupil-work and individual re-teaching was done in the same way as group-work, that is, always beginning with Row One and giving patient instruction, and ending with the last row in a terrible rush to be ready for the recess or lunch-time dismissal bell. Inevitably being called last, low-status pupils had plenty of time to practise and perfect their mistakes, for which they were loudly harangued.

The result of all this was that the English-speaking white children got more and superior teaching at times of the day when they were more alert than did the children from visible racial and ethnic minorities. Soon, the lower groups fell far behind, and patterns similar to those noted earlier by Rist were evident in this class as well. Some children (in one case for misbehaviour) were demoted to lower groups, but lower-group children never moved up: even if their ability might have justified it, their progress through the curriculum was so much slower than that of Group One pupils that they would not have been able to jump the rapidly-growing gap of words, concepts, number, facts, and other prerequisite knowledge yet to be acquired. Sometimes when a Portuguese-speaking child didn't answer the question (in most cases it seemed to be because the child didn't know what answer Miss Smith wanted, and was terrified of getting it wrong) Miss Smith would rephrase the question loudly in pidgin Spanish.

Stratification by racial, ethnic, and linguistic minority mem-bership took place *very* rapidly, and once this had happened, Miss Smith's teaching and controlling activities simply gave rise to the inferiority in performance that she had initially expected. Sorting and selecting, as Parsons had earlier postulated, had taken place within five days! But the 'resistance' that Anyon had observed was nowhere to be seen – they wouldn't dare! As noted in another context by Sharp and Green, the power-difference between the pupils on the one hand, and the teacher on the other precluded this: the typical reactions were earnest conformity on the part of those selected to do well, and resignation and apathy on the part of the others.

If the Pedersens seemed to be blaming Miss Smith, that was not their intention. But blaming the children would be blaming the victims. However, the point is not whether or not to blame; it is rather to understand and to improve. Miss Smith is clearly a victim of certain circumstances, too. Those circumstances need to be changed. But in the meantime, the children suffer, and so does Miss Smith, because she seems to recognise and deeply regret her failure. (On the recognition of the failure on the part of teachers to live up to their own expectations, see McPherson, 1972.)

In describing Miss Jones's situation, it will become clear that, if her teaching seems to be more positive, so do her circumstances. Unlike Miss Smith, Miss Jones's teaching experience was not all at one school, and although currently in favour of teaching in what she called the 'traditional classroom' had previously worked in the 'open classroom' and in teams with other teachers. Miss Jones welcomed visitors – mainly, it seemed, in order to take advantage of them as additional resources to apply to the needs of her students – and was a participant in an experimental language programme with the advice and assistance of helping expert personnel who frequently made unscheduled classroom visits to demonstrate various techniques. In addition, she had an aide, and there was usually a student teacher in the classroom as well. Parents made frequent visits, and were made to feel welcome.

On the first day of school, the children straggled in by ones and twos, usually with a parent in tow, or vice versa. The teacher invited the pupils to go over to the play area – a substantial part of the classroom which she had fitted out with an attractive rug, beautiful books and interesting toys. When Miss Jones felt that a child might not have friends, she introduced that child to some other pupil before turning her attention to the parent. Children were encouraged to interact, for, as Miss Jones told the observers, she thought that they could learn much from one another. In fact, what would have been regarded as 'cheating' in Miss Smith's class was encouraged under most circumstances, and was considered 'being helpful'. Control never seemed to be a problem, and if and when Miss Jones wanted the attention of all the children, she simply and quietly asked for it. The students responded immediately.

If children needed some correction or instruction about either their social behaviour or academic work, it was given in a friendly, kindly, and above all, private manner. Miss Jones did not expect misbehaviour, and when it happened, she seemed genuinely surprised. Her disapproval was always of the misbehaviour, and never of the child.

In the early days, before formal lessons began, there was much talk, discussion, story-telling and many poems and songs. The seating at first was in formal rows, but the plan like the grouping kept changing throughout the year. On some occasions, one or two children would decide to attend all groups, and this was not discouraged. Miss Jones was aware of the need to give equal time to the groups, which she would call in random and unpredictable order. She would occasionally use a kitchen timer with a bell to make sure she was being fair to all.

The socio-economic-status range of the children's families was broader than in Miss Smith's class, and the racial-ethnic mix was richer and more varied. There seemed to be no particular racial or ethnic pattern to the groups, even though some individual children seemed to be much more ready for Grade One than others.

Children loved talking to Miss Jones, and she seemed to have a special personal relationship with each one over and above the teaching role. She listened to them, not for repetitions of her stock answers, but with apparent genuine interest in their ideas and concerns. Loving relationships developed in this atmosphere, not only between the children and the teacher, but among the children themselves. All of the children were treated respectfully by the teacher, and they copied this in their attitudes towards one another as well as towards the student teachers, the language supervisor, the aide, the principal (of whom they seemed especially fond) and the researchers. Even the use of snacks in this classroom contrasted to that of Miss Smith's. Miss Smith occasionally promised the children treats later in the day if they had been good. Miss Jones, on the other hand, offered juice and snacks at times when attention spans were getting short.

Miss Jones enjoyed a number of advantages not available to Miss Smith. We already mentioned the presence of other adults in Miss Jones's classes throughout her career, but there were other factors. Even though there was a socio-economic background range of the children in Miss Jones's classes, which is usually considered a disadvantage by teachers, the availability of some pupils with home backgrounds particularly relevant to a given discussion was used to the advantage of all the pupils. The constant presence of a caring and helping principal was an advantage. But it seemed to be Miss Jones's genuine love and respect for each child that made her find the better ways of teaching.

All the above is not to say that academic stratification did not occur in Miss Jones's class. By the end of the year, many of the pupils were reading at advanced grade three levels, whereas some others were barely at the level expected for grade one, according to their performance on standardised tests. But the class mean score was far in excess of the norms, which is remarkable for an inner-city 'problem' school: furthermore, the obvious pleasure that most of the children took in school work, and the pride they developed in their own achievement demonstrated that it is not necessary to sacrifice social and moral development to academic achievement.

Finally, it was interesting to note that the stratification of the children on the reading scores did *not* coincide with race and ethnicity, as in Miss Smith's class, but seemed rather to reflect perceptible differences in pupils' current general knowledge and reading readiness. The reproduction of the neighbourhood social system seemed to occur in Miss Smith's class, but not in that of Miss Jones. Perhaps Miss Jones was doing some of the things that Miss A had done. The researchers have recently visited Miss Jones's former pupils in the Second Grade classroom at the end of their year, and judging from their current reading scores, general achievement, and inter-personal behaviour, they seem to continue to build on the advantages of the good start they received in Grade One. Incidentally, their Grade Two teacher is a friend of Miss Jones' who shares much of her philosophy of education.

Miss Smith's pattern showed some detailed ways in which what Parsons had hypothesised actually came about, and paralleled the Rist observations to a remarkable degree. However, Miss Jones demonstrated that *these things need not happen.* (The authors have since observed two more teachers in the same way in another large North American city, and it is clear that Miss Jones is not unique in her good effects on children.)

Conclusion

Schooling does not have to be insulting to minority-group pupils. What teachers believe and do in the classroom has enormous potential for influencing the quality of life of their

students. There is now enough evidence of this in the literature that we cannot be indifferent to the importance of schooling and of teachers in the process.

Nearly monocultural countries like Denmark and Iceland are rare in a world where there has historically and recently been so much international and intercontinental migration. Certainly Britain and North America have large populations of people who, because of cultural and physical differences are visibly different from those whose ancestors arrived earlier. Britain and North America are, like it or not, multicultural societies. Even if new arrivals were welcomed with open arms and complete equality, they would still not wish to be 'assimilated'. Despite its long adherence to a political philosophy of America as the 'melting pot of the world', the United States has in recent years acknowledged that it is a multicultural society by its efforts to integrate neighbourhoods and schools, by encouraging instruction in Spanish in state schools, by sponsoring ethnic festivals, and the like. Canada has a Minister of Multiculturalism. This new awareness of a much older truth is undoubtedly here to stay for some time.

A racist, multicultural society is an unjust society, and in the long run, injustice hurts the perpetrators as well as the victims. A just multicultural society values the contributions made by all of its citizens, and respects their differences. In such a society there would be no reason to want to 'assimilate' people into a single culture, nor would there be any sense in trying to make everyone resemble everyone else like so many clones of a 'national ideal type'.

In the context of a larger world where most light-skinned Europeans and Americans are substantially wealthier than most darker-skinned Africans, Asians and others, any society with more than a sprinkling of visibly different people tends to mirror global racism. Nevertheless, there is no more a 'black problem' in Britain and North America than there was a 'Jewish problem' in Nazi Germany. Such 'problems' are clearly in the eyes of the beholders, and the onus of change is not on the victims of discrimination, but rather on those who have learned to discriminate.

Social learning takes place within the larger society, and state schooling, a relatively recent development, is only one of many sources of learning. Classical literature from times before schooling was universal, contains many samples of discrimination on racial, ethnic and religious grounds, as Shakespeare's

Shylock will illustrate. People who grow up in a racist society absorb racism from their daily contacts with even its best elements. However, the existence of schools for all offers an opportunity either to intensify or undermine the learning of prejudice and discrimination. It seems that much harmful interpersonal behaviour is unintended and unconscious. If well-meaning people, who undoubtedly constitute the vast majority in any society, can be shown that certain of their social actions hurt others, they may try to change – especially those such as teachers who have undertaken to work in the helping professions.

Social reforms are needed in all the institutions of modern, multicultural societies, including education. Only when schooling becomes appropriate for all will it be suitable for members of *either* minority or majority groups.

5 Anti-racism, the Economy and Changing Post-sixteen Education

Godfrey Brandt

There are now more young people unemployed in Britain than there have been for at least three decades (Table 1) and there is a percentage increase every year, a pattern of increase which is not dissimilar to that of the general workforce.

This growing unemployment, despite statements made by various state agencies, is not merely a product of the recession but more specifically because of the crisis within the British economy.[1] Yet, ironically, all the attempts within the last decade to 'revive' the economy have been made at the price of massive unemployment. This is exemplified by the stress of the current government on bringing down inflation; on productivity; on monetarism. As Table 1 shows, a higher and rising percentage of young people between the ages of sixteen and nineteen are becoming unemployed, though up to 390,000 of those missing from current percentage figures are on temporary YTSs.

My premise in this chapter is that, on close examination, it will be seen that a disproportionate amount of these unemployed young people will be found to be black. This phenomenon represents the coming together of a network of oppressive structures – racism, capitalism, sexism and generational control – to name the most significant. Education has had and continues to have a major part to play in these structures of oppression and at the transitional stage of education the intrinsic tensions ripen.

One of the projects set up to look at this transitional stage was the Council of Europe's Education Division Project No. 1 and in December 1982 this project was completed with a range of publications and a four-page declaration which more or less

Table 1

Unemployed Young People 16–19			October/January	
	Greater London		United Kingdom	
	No.	% Increase	No.	% Increase
1979	21,134	–	266,900	–
1980	40,116	90	454,100	70
1981	68,115	70	613,500	35
1982	54,388		603,609	
1983	64,795		634,633	
1984	62,909		608,900	
1985 (Jan)	58,642		571,700	

Source: Department of Employment and Greater London Council Statistics
The percentage increases relate to the previous year's figures. This could not
be done with the figures of 1982 and 1983 since the systems of counting and
recording changed in each of those years.

summarised the agreements on the issues identified by the
twenty-one country working party. This project, initiated in
1978, had a specific brief to study the transition from school to
work in Europe with special reference to vocational training.
The declaration was adopted by the DES and as a result, in
March 1983 a conference was convened in this country – the
second country in Europe to organise one after the end of
Project No. 1 – to disseminate and deliberate the contents and
the preoccupations of the working papers.

In opening this conference, Maitland Stobart, head of the
Council's School Education Division, concluded his speech
with four challenges: (i) unemployment and the new technologies; (ii) youth guarantee (i.e. assured work or further
study at the end of secondary school); (iii) answering the
growing challenges to democratic values; (iv) multicultural
society in a changing Western Europe.

This chapter, to some extent, addresses all of these challenges,
especially as they relate to black young people. I attempt to
examine the movements within the changing educational
sphere. Within this complicated network of issues and phenomena, I examine some of the elements that perpetuate the

oppression and exploitation of all youth, but black youth in particular. These deliberations have implications for teachers, further education lecturers, youth workers, careers officers, YTS supervisors and others working within the growing complex of agencies involved in sixteen to nineteen education. Neutrality is not an option – one is either colluding with the oppressive and racist structures operating in education and training or alternatively attempting to oppose them.

Sixteen to Nineteen Education – Historical and Conceptual Backdrop

There is now no question of the mushrooming significance of the MSC as an agent and instrument of change in sixteen to nineteen education and training. This change has given it increased power within the educational sphere. Therefore in this chapter there will be a relatively close examination of its work.

However, before looking more closely at the current work of the MSC and its involvement in the education and training of youth in the transitional stage from school to work (or non-work), it is important to locate it within the context of post-secondary education initiatives and vocational preparation schemes that preceded the MSC's 'New Training Initiative'.

The Historical Setting

The Further Education Unit (FEU) uses a model that places vocational preparation as the third strand of a tri-partite tertiary education (cf. Figure 1). As they outline very well, 'the existing education and training provision for the 16–19 age group can be divided into three categories not necessarily related to conventional intelligence or capability' (FEU, 1981).

Figure 1

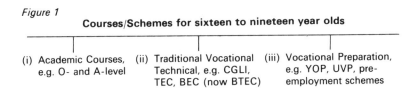

Courses/Schemes for sixteen to nineteen year olds

| (i) Academic Courses, e.g. O- and A-level | (ii) Traditional Vocational Technical, e.g. CGLI, TEC, BEC (now BTEC) | (iii) Vocational Preparation, e.g. YOP, UVP, pre-employment schemes |

These strands represent the continuing selectivity of the British education system and demonstrate an almost complete replication of the old tri-partite system in secondary education which comprehensive education was intended to supplant.

This chapter will focus on the third strand (vocational preparation) in view of its increasing importance and emphasis. Indeed, this is having the greatest impact on the majority of young people and thus the tremendous changes taking place within it have important implications not only for the teaching profession but for the allied professions as well.

Any close examination of the clientele of these three strands will no doubt endorse the fact that strands (ii) and (iii) represent the majority of young people and within that majority there is an over-representation of working-class and black young people. *Ipso facto*, strand (i) is dominated by middle-class youth – as affirmed by Halsey *et al.* (1980), 'the middle class always win'. Therefore when one talks about 'vocational preparation' and youth one is normally talking about a predominantly working-class and disproportionately black group.

The FEU report in reference to this third strand highlights this point:

> In contrast to those following academic or traditional vocational/technical courses, these young people have not normally been selected on the grounds of level of previous attainment, or assumed destination, but they are generally those who remain after selection for the other two groups has taken place (1981).

Nevertheless, though there is an element of truth in the FEU statement, what we are examining is not an error of omission but acts of commission, mainly state manipulation, socio-economic and social reproduction and state and societal institutional racism. (These points will be taken up later.) The focus needs to be 'marginalisation' rather than 'selection', 'racism' rather than 'disadvantage'. These structures continue to work even after this group has been separated out.

Unified Vocational Preparation (UVP)

In July 1976, the government published a statement, 'Unified Vocational Preparation: A pilot approach' which among other things included a recognition by the government of the day that vocational preparation began before young people left school or found jobs. 'The school's role in providing general education and certain basic skills represented only one aspect of this process; employers and the further education and training services also had a part to play' (Wray-Jamieson *et al.*, 1980). The UVP scheme was intended, in a bringing together of these agencies, to provide a meaningful vocational preparation for young people who had already made the transition from school to work (cf. Figure 2). The UVP was to go through numerous changes though it seems it had an inbuilt obsolescence in view of the escalating rate of youth unemployment.

Figure 2

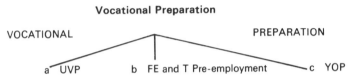

The background of the setting up of the UVP scheme begins with the publication of the Schools' Council report (1972) on careers education. This precipitated the DES report (1973) *Careers Education in Secondary Schools*. These deliberations coincided with the raising of the school leaving age from fifteen to sixteen.

In 1974 an interdepartmental group had been established involving the departments of Education and Science, and Employment and the MSC in order to oversee UVP activities, and in April the following year, HM Inspectorate set up a working party under E. W. Sudale to review sixteen to nineteen provision for those not involved in organised post-secondary school education or training. Particular attention was to be given to the existing provision within further education or training establishments which combined elements of education and training which were apparently successful in motivating young people. In March 1976 the Sudale Report on *Curricula for non-participant 16–19s* was published. This report spelled out guidelines for the development of vocational preparation schemes. These guidelines had the commitment of the government of the day and included the aims of:

(i) Improving, extending and diversifying young people's skills and knowledge, communicative capacity, general understanding and powers of appraisal, extrapolation and application.

(ii) Helping young people to make decisions, develop responsible attitudes, extend their creativity and to overcome disadvantage.

In that same year the City and Guilds of London Institute (CGLI) devised five schemes designed to 'meet' these demands within the following six curriculum areas: (i) industrial and environmental studies; (ii) skills and practices; (iii) technology theory and practice; (iv) communication studies; (v) optional activities; (vi) careers education.

Pre-employment Courses

Pre-employment courses fall more firmly into the category of 'traditional' vocational preparation course; they are usually organised by a college with the support of the relevant LEA and may involve a validating body for part(s) of the course. Students on these courses are usually in the sixteen to nineteen age group and normally attend the college full-time. The course duration is usually a year and normally includes a 'basic educational component' plus a range of vocational options. Students are mainly 'unqualified' and usually have one-day-a-week placements in local firms as work experience. Students are given financial assistance with fares and lunches – small grants being reserved for those with 'special' needs. Some study part-time (i.e. up to twenty-one hours) and are thus able to claim benefit.

The FEU, commissioned by the DES, is currently co-ordinating a programme of support for a series of pilot schemes for the new Certificate of Pre-Vocational Education (CPVE) which started officially in September 1985. This new certificate will replace the various pre-vocational qualifications with a single recognised qualification covering the whole spectrum of needs. The rhetoric that goes with it is that this will be a widely credible qualification acceptable to young people, employers and the public at large. However, this does mark a further centralisation based on a series of assumptions, including ones about the nature and composition of a 'common core curriculum' for post-sixteen pupils. At the time of writing, the evaluation of these schemes is yet to be completed.

The Youth Opportunities Programme

The Youth Opportunities Programme (YOP) has dominated the sixteen to nineteen educational/training arena for the last

five years. This has been through project-based work experience, training workshops, community service schemes and
work experience on employers' premises (WEEP). These YOP
placements, normally made through the Careers Service (with
the approval of the MSC), have been used in a range of
businesses, predominantly small local firms, though they have
included playgroups and other community education agencies.

The 'trainees' (as they were called) on YOP were generally
not academic, but may have had a few O-levels. They spent six to
twelve months on a placement, spending one day per week
attending college, and were supervised by the further education
college staff in conjunction with 'supervisors' provided by the
firm. Each trainee was paid an allowance and a fee was paid to
the college concerned for staffing materials and overheads by the
Training Services Department (TSD).

This is the scenario and the background out of which the YTS
was born and by September 1982, the further education sector
found that increasingly their funding was not coming from the
DES or the LEA, as the case might be, but instead from the
MSC. The MSC was not only becoming more involved in
sixteen to nineteen education/training but was gaining more
control and power over training and the basis on which it took
place.

Education and the Economy

The Transition from School to Work or Non-Work

The liberal tradition of British educational policy has ideologi-
cally portrayed education as the great equaliser and a necessary
precipitate for social mobility. In the functionalist tradition,
education (and thus certification) acts as a mechanism for
rationally selecting and allocating individuals to their future
roles in society and, particularly, into the occupational structure. It matches talents, skills and capacities to the jobs for
which they are most suitable. Schools are thus seen as teaching
the kind of cognitive skills and capacities essential for the
performance of those jobs. Intertwined in these considerations
is the question of the relationship between education and skills;
training and the economy.

There are a number of contingent questions, however, that
must be asked, such as: What is meant by skill? What is the level

of skill necessary for a specific job and who determines this? What is the relationship between education, training and industry? What part does schooling play in the ideological and hegemonic functions implicit in education or training in contemporary British society?

At times of economic boom, these questions, though important, seldom surface. In a time of crisis, they are unavoidable. The raising of the school leaving age, an important example, at each instant was catalysed not necessarily by working-class pressure or ruling-class conscience, but by economic expediency in times of economic crisis.[2] These moves also tend to be accompanied by a political rhetoric conveniently based on notions of 'personal improvement' and 'the national good'.

This 'national good' is usually related to improving the 'health' of the economy for the benefit of all and, therefore, speaks of the need for a workforce trained to help in building the nation's economy through a skilled contribution to industry. Also, the raising of the school leaving age seems to be more related to the elongation of 'youth' as a reserve army of labour and the containment of possible 'rebellion', than with an improved education for effective social mobility.[3]

Having raised the school leaving age to what might be called a threshold of acceptability, the state is in a position where it needs to find alternative ways of creating the same net effect of containment, control and of maintaining a reserve army of labour. The fact that there are now over three million people unemployed and that some 50–60 per cent are under twenty-five years old, is not a 'problem' for the state. What is a problem, is that either these people should *violently* object or, alternatively, lose touch with the work ethic and get out of, or not even acquire, the habit of work. Consequently, alongside the strengthening of the state 'offensive', there is a strengthening of what is euphemistically referred to as 'training opportunities', though one may well ask the question: training for what?

There is a strong ideological connection, within the hegemony of the 'meritocratic' state, between educational achievement and the economy. The relationship is purported by this liberal meritocratic school of thought as educational achievement equals occupational status equals productivity; the underlying principle being that education is free to all, and, therefore, each has the opportunity of 'achieving' all there is to achieve within the society. Yet one might argue that this particularly voluntaristic approach to achievement, social mobility and the economy is much too narrow to be at all useful as an analysis of the structural connection between schooling and the social division of labour. The stress on the individual (the micro) disregards society as a whole (the macro) but, above all, disregards the economic base of society.

There have been several studies done which show a continuing under-representation of working-class and black children in the 'upper streams' (exam classes) in secondary schools (Halsey et al., op. cit.). This phenomenon sets in motion a downward trend along the road of deskilling,[4] and a move towards the creation of a menial labour force, either to perform or to stay in reserve to respond to the dictates of capital.

In this recession, what young people are faced with is a growing situation of 'credential amplification', whereby employers can and are demanding higher academic qualifications for increasingly deskilled jobs. As Lea and Young write (1982), 'this produces a concertina effect on the opportunity structure for school leavers . . . the very links between school certification and occupational achievement which the "Great Debate" was concerned to strengthen are decisively broken.' Though this phenomenon of credential amplification is related more to increased employer power over a labour supply that far outweighs the current needs of capital, it tends to be portrayed by the state as the 'fault' of the youth – a lack of significant training; inappropriate dress; unsuitable attitudes. The state's remedy is then seen in terms of training and retraining both in manual skills and 'social and life' skills. The practical implication is an extension of the educational life of young people, of their 'youth', and of their lack of independence.

There is no real state acknowledgment that youth unemployment is increasingly a structural necessity in a 'mixed' economy. Instead, there are initiatives taken which have the net effect of blaming youth unemployment on 'faulty' supply rather than demand; a failure of the educational system, rather than capitalism; a personal problem of joblessness due to lack of motivation, experience or skill rather than the position youth labour occupies in the market economy.

The creation of the MSC relates quite closely to these specific functions which continue to adjust to the dictates of capital and political expediency. These functions can be divided into two main spheres – the economic and the ideological – each as varied as the other in its hidden and manifest functions.

The Current Scenario

As reported in *The Times Educational Supplement*, 15 July 1983:

> A leading tertiary college is being pushed into cutting its mainstream
> student provision to make up the heavy losses it faces on the Youth
> Training Scheme. Its education authority is refusing to risk
> government penalties by providing the college with the extra money
> it needs.

The writer goes further to emphasise that colleges all over the
country have come to rely on MSC income to cover the cost of
special courses and to provide some 'profit' to subsidize general
provision. But under Mode B2, colleges will be getting only a
fraction of what is being paid to industry for placements, or of
what was paid to them under previous schemes. None of the
options open to this particular college seemed appealing;
namely cutting back on student intake; cutting certain A-level
courses; cutting staff; freezing appointments, or a combination
of these.

Within the current scenario what is becoming much clearer is
that the funding for post-sixteen education and training is being
transferred from one pocket to another. While there are
increasing cuts in the funding of traditional educational services, there is an increase in MSC funding; while these cuts are
decreasing university places, the state is moving towards
creating more places on YTSs (cf. Table 2).[5]

Further, in Circular 6/82 (DES, 1982, para 5) the DES makes
clear its acceptance that the responsibility for ensuring the
delivery of such programmes as YOP and UVP should rest with
the MSC. Therefore, 'accordingly, in order to simplify lines of
responsibility' (ibid.) the management of UVP was transferred
to the MSC. This circular announced the establishment of what
was considered to be a 'strong' consultative committee involving the MSC, the education departments and the LEAs. This
consultative committee was set up to succeed the interdepartmental group in anticipation of the setting up of a YTS
which was intended to cater for both the employed and
unemployed young people aged sixteen plus.

The assertions of this Circular 6/82 mark the abdication
of the DES as the department responsible for education in
deference to an ascendant MSC. This educational restructuring
is evident not only within the sixteen to nineteen age group but
within the fourteen to sixteen age group – the upper end of

Table 2

Expenditure (in millions) in secondary/further/higher education and in the MSC (Training Budget)

	1979–80	1980–1	1981–2	1982–3	1983–4
Schools (All)	5,431	5,110	4,716	4,820	4,720
Further and Higher Education	2,617	2,643	2,482	2,410	2,370
Universities	837	864	814	*796	*770
MSC (Training Budget)		498.3	690.2	812.6	1,181.4
MSC (Youth Training Scheme)		213.7	395.5	542.9	771.1

Source: These figures are based on material from the MSC Annual Report 83/4 and the Government Expenditure Plans of March 1980/1 – March 1983/4

* These figures are approximations based on figures from the Expenditure Plans.

secondary – who are about to be the involuntary participants of the TVEI which is now at its pilot stage. One of the major, stated purposes of this scheme is to select out the 'best' pupils for skills training in the new technologies.

What becomes very clear on looking more closely at the broad issues of 'youth' training is that there is an emergent and growing state pre-occupation with sixteen to nineteen year olds. This 'youth' cateogory is, however, being extended both ways to include from fourteen year olds to twenty-five year olds. This constituency, it is being argued, despite the employment situation, needs more training opportunities, but the 'traditional' agencies seem to be inadequate to perform this function. Instead, the state is employing more and more the 'skills' and 'expertise' of the MSC. The question is why? Davis's (1981) response is that this phenomenon has implications which extend beyond the prima facie argument that, 'at school young people have often been less well prepared than they should for working life'. It seems that any response to this question of why, must be a complex one – based on an analysis of restructuration. In the vanguard of this restructuration is the MSC.

Why the MSC? – the Rationale

On closer examination the dual ideological/economic function which the MSC has to perform is evident. These two functions overlap and are sometimes indistinguishable from each other. The opening paragraphs of the Youth Task Group Report categorically disavow any connection between the MSC and the government's economic policy. Yet in providing a substantial post-sixteen education, it ensures that the dominant considerations in education and training of youth are not 'educational' but economic, since the MSC's New Training Initiative is seen as an economic solution as opposed to an educational one. The problems perceived by the MSC with the British economy as presented in the 1981 *A New Training Initiative*, could be summarised in terms of a need to be competitive within the European market, and in so doing to exploit the new technologies which are becoming available. This analysis acknowledges that the world economy is in a 'period of transition', whereby new countries are becoming industrialised and thus providing additional competiton with which Britain cannot vie unless major changes are made.

The internal dynamics are analysed in terms of the gradual disappearance of low skilled and manufacturing jobs and the increase in the service sectors, which creates the need for a more highly skilled workforce.

Because firms do not have a sufficiently skilled workforce or the resources to provide adequate training, they cannot cope with change. On the other hand, apprenticeships are seen to be inadequate in that they provide too few opportunities for girls outside the traditional female occupations.

With regard to the issue of training, it is argued that there is not enough opportunity for further education and training in Britain, in contrast to Britain's European competitors; that there is, in fact, a drop in new skill training opportunities and that training is bedevilled by the wrong view of what training is about.

The net effect, they argue, is that school leavers are unprepared for working life.

Despite its liberal rhetoric, the MSC, as I have argued above, is involved in an industrial conscription of young people which is amounting to, among other things, another raising of the school-leaving age. The Commission also seems to be involved in creating a mass labour force of 'deskilled' workers. As stated by the Task Group, their aim is 'to develop and maintain a more versatile, readily adaptable, highly motivated and productive workforce'. While there are cuts in education and in places for young people in universities and colleges, there is a concomitant increase in MSC funds and projects, and this serves to polarise youth along class and academic lines. Instead of vertical mobility they offer 'horizontal' mobility[6] based on a notion of the 'sincere' desire to work.

The stress on social and life skills attempts not only to keep the work ethic alive, but to place the blame for unemployment again with the victims. At the same time, the MSC's analysis of a mismatch between schooling and the economy helps to justify its own existence, as well as the increasing cuts in education. This reduces the culpability of the state, while expiating its guilt.

Therefore, YTS seems to be the single most important phenomenon in the sphere of sixteen to nineteen education and the TVEI is an important washback effect. Thus TVEI must also be viewed critically. Professor Malcolm Skilbeck commenting on this fourteen to eighteen initiative, which was only at its pilot stage insisted that it is,

a direct attack on the principles underpinning comprehensive education. A diagnosis which results in crash courses in vocational preparation at an early age and a division of the school population into academic and vocational cannot be accepted, whatever the power of its proponents or the resources at their disposal (*The Times Educational Supplement*, 15 July 1983).

MSC – Underlying Functions

As distinct from its rhetoric, the MSC seems to function in certain distinct ways, the least of which is an injection of further subsidy into a flagging British industry through providing an 'incentive' to employers to take on young people under the new scheme.

In fact, under the old YOP scheme one Cornish farmer wrote to his MP expressing great regret that he had not received one of the 'free boys'. Now under the YTS these 'boys' are not only free but the employer/sponsor get £1,850 per trainee per year with an additional £100 pounds fee per training place paid to those who manage an entire programme. Also, in general, if employers train three additional trainees for every two they would normally recruit, they will receive a grant of £1,850 for each of the five young people recruited. Thus industry has the guarantee of cheap labour for as long as it chooses to take advantage of it, even though the stated intention is that industry should take over the scheme in full. These employment schemes have been likened to industrial conscription – a conscription that would, one would imagine, be a very welcome practice for British industry. Yet initially industry seemed somewhat reluctant to take on young people on the YTS scheme – especially the larger firms and particularly in the case of black young people.

The question is why? Was there a discrepancy between the government's insights concerning the perceived needs of industry and the perceptions of industry *per se*? The fact is that despite the stress on 'quality', YTS had limited capacity to provide 'skills' in one year (especially in relation to the new technologies), though it had tremendous capacity to deskill. Thus it is not surprising that in his spring budget of 1985 the Chancellor of the Exchequer, Nigel Lawson, announced the extension of YTS to a two-year programme. Yet even this initiative is two pronged since, as Biddy Passmore (*The Times Educational Supplement*, March 1985) comments, 'If the Cabinet also decides to scrap supplementary benefit for 16 and 17 year olds who refuse to join the scheme, unemployment in the under 18s will be effectively wiped out.'

However, despite the trend at the beginning of the scheme of Mode A YTS trainees being taken on mainly by small firms, the larger firms seem to be re-assessing their original tendency not to take on trainees. Yet one can expect continued selectivity, since big businesses, like the banks, know that they can have exactly the 'quality' of trainee they desire. As stated in *The Times Educational Supplement* (Jackson, 15 July 1983), 'The banks have a simple method,' he said [i.e. Jack Mansell, FEU director]. 'You've got to have 6 O-levels to get on their YTS. That's the reality.'

Because of the reluctance and 'choosiness' of industry, the majority of YTS places have been in further education establishments and of the Mode B2 variety, though young people have been very reluctant in taking up these places. In addition to resorting to Mode B2, the government in its desperation has even attempted to initiate an army scheme – a scheme which one might argue signals a conscription of a more obvious type.

The army scheme was greeted with considerable reluctance and as reported in the educational press:

The services have rejected the idea of dropping these standards [i.e. normal army standards] for the unemployment trainees because they hope to use the scheme in the same way as many firms are planning to use YTS – as a way of trying out possible permanent recruits for a year at the expense of the MSC (*The Times Educational Supplement*, 12 August 1983).

This scheme, which has variously been seen as strongly connected to the specific social control intention of youth employment schemes, was disbanded due to lack of take-up, in 1985. Thus the attempt to colonise young people in the absence of real jobs could be seen as having failed.

In addition to the 'control' function exemplified in the attempt at an army scheme, these schemes can also be seen as having an important role in extending the dependence of youth and deferring their entry into the job market in the light of the ever-rising structural unemployment levels, thus masking the true unemployment figures as suggested by Passmore (op. cit.). Of course, they could also be seen as operating to maintain a reserve army of labour through, among other things, keeping the work ethic alive.

This is done through elements of the schemes such as 'Social and Life Skills' programmes which stress the accepted behaviours of industry and inculcate an acceptance of the behavioural norms concomitant with an adherence to the hierarchical structures of line management. On the other hand, the MSC sent out a letter (later withdrawn) demanding that MSC funded courses should not include any sort of political education or any work that is critical of the MSC or government policy. Though this letter was withdrawn, it made explicit the implicit role of the MSC – that of control and containment.

In an economy with full employment, work experience 'schemes' are unnecessary save to enhance the smooth transition from school to work. Current special training programmes seem to be a mere cosmetic. With full employment, firms can provide their own training. Schools have adapted and can continue to do so in response to new demands being made upon them, but no amount of training will provide new jobs for anyone when there are no jobs to be had. By the same token, to give training to wait for an upturn in the economy is waiting for an economic 'pie in the sky'.

Current economic projections for the future suggest that, even with an alternative economic strategy, structural un-

employment will remain at a relatively high rate. As Chris Ellis
states:

> The continuing failure of the job market to provide openings for
> young people has consequences which are accumulative. The nature
> of the problem makes it impossible to solve by relying exclusively on
> job-related services – careers advice, retraining and subsidised
> work experience – because they all presuppose that there is a job to
> be found at the end of the day (Ellis, 1980, p. 17).

The implications of this observation are articulated by the
authors of *Unpopular Education* in this way:

> Under the impact of the economic crisis and the non-so-great-
> education-debate, a new tripartite system of provision for 16–19 year
> olds has hardened into shape: sixth form colleges for the academic
> élite who will occupy various kinds of managerial positions in
> society, full-time education and technical training for those who will
> operate the new technologies and YOPs and a host of similar
> schemes for the reserve army of youth who will perform a servicing
> role – if they get jobs at all (CCCS, 1981).

Impact on Young People

There is a tremendous impact on young people due to this
current focus/emphasis on training of the sixteen to nineteen
age group both in educational and industrial terms. The trend
seems to show that while more young people are pushed into
manual-skills training, university and other 'high status' education will be restricted to a small élite. The Education Secretary
(Sir Keith Joseph) stated in a letter to Sir Edward Parkes,
outgoing chairman of the University Grants Committee, that he
was unable to give any undertaking that current levels of
spending will be preserved (*Guardian*, 12 September 1983). Yet
there is a simultaneous move towards a 'youth guarantee' in
government policy that says there is a guaranteed YTS place for
young people between the ages sixteen and nineteen, which the
government hopes will be extended. At the same time, as
mentioned before, in September 1985 there were 80,000
places made available on the new CPVE courses.

Continuing Inequalities

It is not very hard to become enwrapped in the vilification of
agencies such as the MSC and their initiatives in training, but

this would not be wholly just. As a quango, the MSC acts semi-autonomously, but ultimately it acts at the behest of the government of the day and in harmony with its economic and political objectives. The fact is, that though the fundamental basis of the MSC may be wrong and based on an erroneous analysis, there are still some positive things that have been done and can be done despite rather than within that framework. However, I would argue that these effects would be profoundly limited, and mostly through the actions of individuals and/or small groups.

As I have emphasised, there are fundamental problems with the economic, educational, political and sociological assumptions of YTSs. In addition there are a number of inequalities perpetuated by racist, sexist and classist practices which work against the best of palliative measures. Thus the already disenfranchised and 'disadvantaged' are further repressed.

For example, there has been a great deal of protest over the arbitrary and artificial age restriction of the schemes. Not only does it exclude a large percentage of unemployed youth (only sixteen year olds are guaranteed a place at present) but has been seen as discrimination against their 'handicapped' counterpart who might take longer to be 'ready' for the scheme. However, to the credit of the MSC, in response to pressure, the arrangements for such young people with 'special needs' have adjusted to offer places to eighteen to twenty-one year olds.

Also, despite the fact that within the rhetoric of the MSC the arrangements for girls in YTS are supposed to include equality of access to every type of activity (in keeping with EEC guidelines), the practice seems to suggest that girls are tending to be placed in traditionally 'female' trades. The government's emergency 'army scheme' initially made no provision for girls – an omission that suggests a perceived lack of urgency and even a possible affirmation of the myth of the male breadwinner in an economic climate that says no such experience will be the lot of most of these young people.

However, I shall now focus on the continuing inequality of these measures within the specificity of the black experience though, as I have already stated, there are profound implications for other groups as well. First of all, black youth are victims of the structural racism which has operated throughout their schooling and within the economic sphere to make sure that they are principally part of that third tier of youth within the post-sixteen 'tri-partite system'. Thus they will tend to be a large percentage of the number competing for YTS placements. But the same structures that operated to keep them out of the 'real' jobs will tend to operate to keep them out of YTS Mode A placements. As Lee and Wrench (1981) identified, in addition to racial discrimination, the structural racism of unequal access to job contact networks and the shift of jobs to the suburbs both operate to create a disproportionate rate of unemployment between black and white youth. Research on YOP has shown that though YOP has had a good record in the recruitment of young blacks (especially of West Indian origin), they were less likely to enter WEEP. Also over the last five years the percentage of blacks as compared to the percentage of whites that went on to jobs has been dropping considerably. In the words of Greaves (MSC Report R & D Series No. 16):

> YOP was therefore found to respond well to the needs of West Indians in terms of entry to the programme but as unemployment rose, was not able to overcome their disadvantage in the labour market and a lower proportion were able to get jobs afterwards compared to whites.

This pattern can be transferred to YTS placements for those three reasons plus others since, as stated in *The Times Educational Supplement*, employers, if they respond at all, can afford to be selective.

> The fact that the scheme was voluntary and that employers had to be persuaded to participate meant that the scheme was bound to be selective. It is just wishful thinking to believe that we can isolate YTS from the society in which we live (Jackson, 15 July 1983).

Thus it seems that of the majority of sixteen year olds who will actually be taking up their place on Mode B2 schemes at a college of further education, a disproportionate percentage will be black. Yet even here, judging from the findings of the evaluation of one pilot project, black youth continue to be marginalised. This pilot scheme in Bedfordshire purported to 'correspond' closely to those elements defined as essential components of the New Training Initiative. At the end of their list of aims they state categorically that the vocational preparation package, 'should have a validity in its own right as a maturing process as well as providing a means of improving job and/or further education prospects'. The scheme was set up on the basis of a 'firm non-rejection policy'. Selection criteria were unspecified and based on the applicants' motivation and ability to learn and not on 'qualification or experience'. The scheme had two strands: Strand I: non-specific training and experience and Strand II: specific training and experience. The former was for the less able and the undecided young people whereas the latter was for those with a 'clear vocational bias and the appropriate aptitude'. But, predictably, in this project the marginalisation of black youths was perpetuated in that the majority of black students/trainees were concentrated in Strand I and about 60 per cent of the black young people involved in Strand II were concentrated in the traditional occupational skill areas – hardly a preparation for the new technologies or, indeed, for employment.

Another example of a different order of the way in which black young people are being relegated to an industrial underclass is the MSC's position regarding a particular London 'Access' programme.

The programme is organised into three components: (i) a basic foundation course; (ii) a twelve-month preparatory course at the local further education college involved with the project; (iii) a four-year business studies degree at the polytechnic involved with the project. This degree includes a sandwich year of a paid placement within industry.

This particular programme, which was partly funded by the MSC, has had the MSC contribution withdrawn as from March 1986. This withdrawal was made because, as the MSC saw it, the scheme was mainly concerned with 'education' rather than 'training for work'. The decision was taken despite the fact that the scheme had the support of employers, a specific vocational purpose and a clear intention of providing a five-year programme aimed at facilitating access to high quality business careers for young adults of 'ethnic minority' backgrounds. (The education authority provided the bulk of funding for the project.)

Having jointly funded the first foundation course, the MSC insisted that the second course should be broadened and generalised to lead the majority of trainees directly into work and 'other' outcomes rather than into further education. In order to obtain the funding this was officially agreed. However, the crux came when the course was a remarkable success in the programme group's terms (i.e. success in going on to the next stage of the programme) but a 'nil placement rate' in the MSC's terms, since the MSC hoped that the majority if not all of the trainees would go straight into employment.

Accordingly, at the time of writing, it seems that it is the MSC's intention to uphold its decision to withdraw funding from the project. This case seems to lend support to the argument that the MSC are more concerned with short-term palliatives than with long-term job opportunities at a high level. This is bound to have a profound effect on young people in general but on black young people in particular.

Conclusion

What I have attempted to establish in this chapter is a general background to the current happenings in the sphere of post-sixteen education especially in relation to the third strand of the tri-partism which has been identified. I have argued that we are in the midst of a restructuring of the education system, especially in this sector, based on a number of motives and interests which may in fact prove to be inimical to the interests of young people. I argue that these moves perpetuate the 'disadvantage' of the 'disadvantaged' black youth more than most. Black youths, therefore, continue to be victims of structural and systematic racism as well as marginalisation which ensures that they remain at the bottom of a heap of dispossessed youth.

Thus in conclusion I would like to emphasise the need for more positive practices in the education of black young people throughout the education system but particularly in the sphere of post-sixteen education and training. These 'positive practices' become even more urgent in the current socio-economic climate in Britain today. Thus education must examine why, despite palliative measures, the education system continues to fail black young people and how they continue to be ill-prepared and ill-equipped to maintain a decent and acceptable (to themselves) life in this society. Hand in hand with this must be a concerted fight against the racism and racist structures that perpetuate this situation. A blind adherence to 'multicultural-ism' is not sufficient.

The education system needs to provide not just positive images but positive practices in the transmission of knowledge and skills, as well as oppositional ones of an anti-racist nature. Thus educators must find ways of working in and with the community at large providing both adults and children with an education for liberation.

These concepts of 'positive practice' and 'education for liberation' are inextricably linked with anti-racist education at every level. However, the implications of these for sixteen to nineteen education are even greater. This is precisely because the restructuring that is taking place in education is at its sharpest here. What is involved is not merely a changing power structure but a diversification. The power and control at this stage of education now rests with the DoE through the MSC plus, to a reduced degree, with the DES and LEAs. In addition, whether active or inactive, industry has a considerable amount of power over the life chances of young people, in that industry is now seen as operating explicitly as an element of the education system. Thus, two levels of struggle must be engaged in by the 'anti-racist' further education lecturer, youth worker, careers officer, school teacher and, of course, the 'on-the-job' MSC supervisor.

One level is that of individual or collective action within one's specific professional context: the second level is collective and co-ordinated action across the range of professional and occupational groups involved in this sphere of education and training.

At the first level, one needs to formulate a position that is effectively what may crudely be defined as 'in and against the state' and anti-racist. This position needs to acknowledge that the current structure of sixteen to nineteen education in this vocational field is fundamentally flawed. As Susannah Lash (1983) asserts, 'until we recognise that and understand why, we will not be able to devise a strategy that gives us any hope of maintaining conditions of service, or of providing schemes of use to "young people".'

At the second level, further education teachers need to look towards their other colleagues involved in this phase of education and together work towards:

(i) The development of a sustained and cogent critique of the basic assumptions of YTS as well as its organisational realisation.
(ii) The confluent formulation of an anti-racist policy with an inbuilt system of evaluation/monitoring.
(iii) The growth of a programme of staff development along these lines as well as the implementation of its ideals.

This youth scenario is cast against a backdrop not only of a general crisis in capital but of an ideological crisis that realises itself in the form of a growing erosion of the rights of workers in general but of state workers in particular. This makes it all the more important that all the workers addressed here combine resources towards a greater understanding of what effect the restructuring of sixteen to nineteen education is having on young people's life chances. It is certain that if the life chances of white young people are at risk, it is even more so for black youth. Therefore this greater shared understanding must lead to nothing less than positive action and counteraction – passivity equals collusion.

NOTES

1 See HALL, S. *et al.* (1978) *Policing the Crisis: Mugging, the State and Law and Order*, chapter 9. London: Macmillan, for a detailed analysis of the 'crisis', especially in relation to the black community.

2 HABERMAS, J. (1975) *Legitimation Crisis.* Boston, MA: Beacon (also 1976; London: Heinemann Educational) provides a useful analysis of the concept of crisis and of the mechanics of legitimation.

3 The changing position and definition of youth is well charted in GILLIS, J. R. (1974) *Youth and History.* New York: Academic Press (revised edition 1981; London: Academic Press).

4 See FRIEND, A. and METCALF, A. (1981) *Slump City.* London: Pluto Press; and BRAVERMAN, H. (1975) *Labour and Monopoly Capital.* New York: Monthly Review Press, for more detailed discussion pertaining to the issues of 'skills' and 'deskilling'.

5 According to Professor Norman Graves in his lecture 'Teacher Education in Adversity' (published by the Institute of Education):

> I take it that I do not need to give much time to establishing that the resources available to universities have declined in absolute terms since 1980, in spite of recent attempts by some in the DES to indicate that no cuts have been imposed (*THES*, 8.2.85). The Government's own White Paper (Cmnd 9143) indicated that since 1980 overall funding for universities has been reduced by 8 per cent in real terms. (Lecture delivered at University of London Institute of Education, Wednesday, 6 March 1985.)

6 The article by Andy Green (1982), 'Education and Training: Under New Masters', is a useful and relevant reference.

6 The School Curriculum

Keith Kimberley

Changing Perspectives on the Curriculum

Among teachers and those who make policy for schools at the level of local and central government, there seems to be a general consensus that the school curriculum should be related both to the present state of society and to hopes for its future and that curricular aims should be framed within this broad agreement. There is, however, far less agreement on how to read, or interpret, the society in which we live, and open disagreement on the values which should inform the future shaping of society.

Not least difficult for those involved in education in the last two decades has been the problem of deciding on the degree of responsiveness to be accorded to diversity. Consider this key statement on the curriculum from the DES in *The School Curriculum* which brings to the foreground these 'issues' as worthy of special mention:

> First, our society has become multicultural; and there is now among pupils a greater diversity of personal values. Second, the effect of technology on employment patterns sets a new premium on adaptability, self-reliance and other personal qualities. Third, the equal treatment of men and women embodied in our law needs to be supported in the curriculum (DES, 1981b).

Now consider this discussion of the complex patterns of attainment of children of different classes and groups by Mortimore and Mortimore written for the ILEA:

> The policy of the ILEA has been to prepare *all* pupils and students for life in what has become a multicultural society, and, whilst taking care not to overemphasize cultural diversity, has sought to build on its strengths. This is in line with the argument that what is needed is a multicultural curriculum which 'is a perfectly natural response to the altered nature of British society and, for many teachers, to the cultural composition of the classes they teach' (ILEA, 1983a).

At one level, the two approaches look similar. They share an assumption which perceives Britain as having *become* multicultural. (This appears to imply that British society was in the past not multicultural until some recent event – presumably the advent in large numbers of visible minorities.) Similarly, they share the use of the term 'multicultural', using it as an umbrella to encompass a variety of dimensions.

At another level, there are substantial differences, as might be expected given the radically different contexts from which the two documents come. By contrast with the DES emphasis on the expression of diversity in terms of *personal* values and the impact of future employment/unemployment patterns on *individuals*, the Mortimores' paper puts emphasis on the preparation of 'all pupils and students for life in a multicultural *society*'. In this they follow the major shift in thinking of the late 1970s which asserted the importance of reviewing the curriculum for *all* students in *all* schools and which in the 1980s has become an organising principle in the Swann Report, *Education for All* (DES, 1985).[1] The ILEA document is also distinct from that of the DES in the implicit acknowledgment that, in the real world, the formulation of policy is concerned with difficult problems of selection and balance. For example, 'Whilst taking care not to overemphasise cultural diversity, has sought to build on its strengths' suggests a practical understanding of the curriculum decision-making process.

The difficult and delicate decisions referred to above affect all teachers and it is both the virtue and the vice of a devolved system of responsibilities for the curriculum that much responsibility is located at the level of the classroom. Teachers, at the time of writing, are particularly aware of pressures on them from a variety of sources, which they ultimately have to resolve in terms of the content they select and the approaches they adopt.

There is increasing pressure from central government as it seeks to exert control over defining the outlines of the curriculum. There is pressure from LEAs for schools to give information to meet DES demands for curriculum statements and the LEAs' own policy requirements. In many areas, there is pressure from parents and community pressure groups to which teachers are often uncertain how to respond. Often teachers are called on to decide between rival proposals for content, or between conflicting interpretations of reality. Sometimes they have to choose between contradictory messages from central government, LEA and local community. This is perhaps what Jenkins and Shipman have in mind when they describe the curriculum in terms of 'transactions' at a 'trading post . . . on the cultural boundary between generations, between sexes, and between cultures' where 'all the value dilemmas of a pluralistic society find their expression . . . This means that the trading post isn't simply on the boundary between generations but also between competing ideologies with society' (Jenkins and Shipman, 1976).

Another way of viewing current concerns is to suggest that the curriculum always has been a point at which conflicting values and competing ideologies in society have been 'magically' resolved – usually in favour of maintaining existing routes to knowledge and privilege. What has changed, perhaps, is the sense of sureness that teachers know what to select from the culture and how to relate what happens in schools to the 'needs' of society. Willey takes this argument further by arguing that:

> The presence of minority ethnic groups in Britain has had the effect of raising questions which have fundamental implications for the very nature of the schooling which is provided. Post-war, black immigration has thrown into sharp relief many of the basic issues inherent in the development of UK education over the last thirty years (Willey, 1982b).

In this view of schooling and hence the curriculum, it is not that society has 'become multicultural' but that the presence of visible and resistant minorities has brought into the open the 'basic issues' which divide society.

Education in and for a Multicultural Society

The difficulties involved in attempts to resolve within the curriculum the conflicting social and economic relationships, attitudes and values which exist in society at large find representation in the very language used. When we talk of educating students 'in and for a multicultural society', the phrase has encoded within it the shifts in perspectives and priorities of recent educational history.

The formula generally used in this book, 'in and for a multicultural society', has the advantage of ensuring that the debate makes problematic the nature of society itself. It makes the focus for re-thinking the curriculum explicit; implies the need for tackling also the institutional structures within which the curriculum is experienced; and raises, though it does not resolve, the tricky relationship between schooling and the 'needs' of society.

The term 'multicultural', despite its useful portmanteau nature, is, however, much limited by its recent history. Classrooms, or schools, have been defined as 'multicultural'. This has meant variously that the teachers thought the self-image of ethnic minority students needed to be supported; that advantage was to be taken of the presence in the classroom of students whose cultural background was different to widen the perspectives of the majority; or, quite crudely, that anyone looking in through the classroom door would see that the class was not predominantly white. Each of these meanings and contexts denies the application of 'multicultural' to *all* classrooms. In the first two of these narrow definitions, 'multicultural' is perceived as a perspective in which the supposed needs of certain ethnic groups provides the organising principle or, when the implications for all children are considered, it is perceived in terms of how children can benefit from encounters with such 'interesting' bits of custom, language or religion as their fellow students can offer. In the third example 'multicultural' has become equated simply with being visibly different.

These usages have created considerable confusion and generated the idea that there actually are kinds of education which can be called 'multicultural' rather than a need for responses within education to the historical and continuing diversity of British society. Equally dangerous has been the implication that the only place where change is needed is in schools where specific ethnic 'minorities' are visibly present. Ethnicity has been proposed solely in terms of the ethnicity of 'minorities'. This has had the effect of preventing people seeing the implications for mainstream culture of contact between languages and cultures and hence of recognising that intercultural contact is reciprocal by nature. Each culture affects and re-shapes others with which it comes into contact. Cultures in contact do not remain static but are subject to continual change.

The 'Multicultural' Curriculum and its Critics

Definitions from within the narrow range referred to above have permeated much curriculum thinking and practice. Units of study added into existing, otherwise unaltered, syllabuses have set out to tell black children the story of 'their' culture, often including uncritically the 'experience' of slavery or stories from 'homelands'. What is horribly clear in retrospect is a marked reluctance to reconceptualise courses as a whole and a tendency to patronise in order to cover over lack of knowledge and understanding. The inclusion, for example, of a special option of Asian and Afro-Caribbean texts at A-level by one examination board was the product of a well-intentioned attempt to respond to diversity, without thinking through possible developments which would benefit all students studying English literature in a society which recognises itself as multicultural. What initially may have seemed a generous gesture towards a specific candidature in so-called 'multicultural' schools can, in retrospect, be seen as calling into question many of the traditional criteria used for selecting English literature texts.

Black critics of what has been generally termed 'multicultural education' have seen in this kind of narrow concentration on the ethnic minority group cultures and histories, and in particular on Afro-Caribbean content, a reflection in the school of the unequal relationship in terms of economic and political power which exists between black and white people in society beyond the school gates. Black parents, teachers, and academics[2] have argued that the attention paid to the cultural background of their children has not paid dividends in terms of examination success and that it has functioned as a means of containing their children's dissatisfactions with their schooling in a racist society.

No amount of talk about culture by teachers has been able to convince black parents that the schools are working well for all their children. They have repeatedly pointed to the failure of the education system to enable their children to do as well as they should numerically in terms of examination results and to enable their children to write accurately in standard English. They have waged a long war of attrition to avoid black students being disproportionately represented in low streams and in special schooling and have challenged the assessment procedures on which such allocations are based. They have wanted to know why black teachers are not more prominent in the schools which their children attend. Many have lost all confidence that the teachers of their children will expect enough from them.

It is also important to point out that the critics of multicultural education include white teachers. A survey conducted by Little and Willey in 1981 found that LEAs and schools which had few or no minority group students predominantly appeared to see the preparation of their students for life in a multicultural society as 'not a matter which concerned them' or suggested that 'positive initiatives would be divisive' (Little and Willey, 1981). These findings were confirmed by Matthews and Fallows in research for the Swann Committee. They noted that:

> Almost without exception, the schools visited saw the concept of multicultural education as remote and irrelevant to their own needs and responsibilities, taking the view that such an approach was needed only where there were substantial numbers of ethnic minority pupils . . . little consideration had been given to the need to amend their work to take account of cultural diversity: indeed such moves were often seen as being too controversial and too inflammatory to contemplate (DES, 1985).

Such statements would appear to be based on a view which assumes that British society is essentially harmonious and just. But there appears also to be a recognition of a threat to this stability if the curriculum were to be influenced by the cultural diversity of society. It is a view which sees society as essentially static and assumes that students' lives will be restricted to specific territorial and cultural frameworks. It is a view based on a myth both about society and about culture.

Redefining Multicultural Education

Aware of the dimensions discussed above and in particular of the need for a rationale for teachers, Davis (1981) has argued that the problem with the earlier forms of multicultural education was that the curriculum proposed was 'based on a cultural racist ideology and not on educational principles'. He points to a prevalent pattern in which curriculum change has been conducted in terms of *content* rather than *concepts*. Since those doing the choosing have been educated themselves within the monocultural curriculum, the content examples have tended to be selected and perceived from the position of the dominant white British culture. Thus, he argues, multicultural education needs to be redefined as the transmission of worthwhile concepts, skills, attitudes, values and principles through the selection of content which is chosen from at least the range of cultures to be found in British society. He is particularly scathing on the subject of 'topics on cultures', asking how any teacher can *do* the West Indies in five weeks and Asian culture in half a term. 'Before teachers do this kind of work they really ought to prepare a five week topic on English culture and having seen the results, should abandon the model' (Davis, 1981). This redefinition of multicultural education offers an answer to those who have been critical of its proponents' failure to face up to the racism inherent in prevailing white ethno-centric perspectives, and in the structures of British society, since for Davis worthwhile concepts, skills, attitudes, values and principles are those which are conceptually strong enough to expose and deal with racism and related inequalities based on sex and class in both personal and institutional contexts. A *multicultural education* then becomes a 'good' education for all students in all places, one that is likely to be based on a re-thinking of all that is taught in relation to its appropriateness and contribution to the development of a more equal, less discriminatory society.

'A Perspective Emphasising Primarily Equality'

What needs to be emphasised at this stage in the argument is that beyond a certain point the re-interpretation of the multicultural paradigm becomes less satisfactory than its replacement by alternative formulations. This is the view expressed in Berkshire's Discussion Paper (1981) which has also been adopted by the ILEA as 'a policy for equality' (ILEA, 1983, c, d, f). In it the specific criticisms from the black community referred to above have been brought together with a more fully developed understanding of what is involved in tackling racism in its structural as well as attitudinal dimensions than was apparent in the late 1970s when the first 'multicultural' policies were framed. What is also apparent in the case of the ILEA is a determination simultaneously to tackle issues concerning class and gender.

In this perspective, the dehumanising effect of racism on white people, giving them distorted views of their identity, society and history, is put alongside the web of discriminatory policies, practices and procedures which constitute institutional racism for black people. Both the ideological and the structural components, it is argued, must be tackled if racism is to be dismantled.

Richardson (1982) elaborates the implications for the curriculum of this perspective. He emphasises the problematic nature of the relation between what goes on in school and the direction taken in society.

Changes in society do not necessarily have to be accepted or
welcomed in schools and neither in schools nor in society should
changes be considered independently of the distribution of power
and, therefore, of questions about whose material interests are being
promoted, and whose are being challenged.

Against the DES (1977b) Green Paper *Education in Schools*
view that the curriculum 'should reflect a sympathetic understanding of the different cultures and races that now make up
our society', he proposes an 'Alternative Green Paper' framed in
the following terms:

> Our society contains conflicts of interest between social classes,
> between the sexes, between generations, between the dominant,
> mainly racist white majority on the one hand and ethnic minorities
> of Asian or Caribbean background on the other. Within world
> society as a whole, Britain's ruling élite is part of the North: it is in
> economic conflict with the South, and actively colludes with and
> benefits from patterns of repression and exploitation in Third
> World countries. As part of the West it is in conflict also with the
> East, and wastes vast sums of money on armaments. The curriculum
> of our schools should help pupils and teachers and the local
> authorities to which they belong, to understand the power struc-
> tures in which they participate as victims or as beneficiaries, and
> should help them develop commitment to, and practical skill in
> working from their various positions towards greater equality, peace
> and justice, locally, nationally and internationally (Richardson,
> 1982).

Policy and Planning

So far in this chapter the discussion has been in terms of shifts of
perception and emphasis and has been of most relevance to the
formulation of aims for the curriculum. This next section
considers responses being made at the levels of DES, LEAs,
examinations boards and schools.

Department of Education and Science Responses

There is little indication at the time of writing in DES
statements on the curriculum that it is yet the central priority for
those taking stock of the curriculum to analyse ways in which the
British version of a multicultural society comes to have such
deeply embedded inequalities based on race, class and gender in

its daily life, ways of thinking and institutional structures. It will be a matter of considerable importance to see in what ways the Secretary of State for Education responds to the recommendation in *Education for All* that:

> The response of schools, both 'multi-racial' and 'all white', to cultural diversity has to be seen as a central feature of the current debate on the balance and breadth of the school curriculum. The Secretary of State should focus on this issue when considering responses to DES Circular 8/83 and in any further statements that he may make and any agreements that he may seek about the curriculum (DES, 1985).

It may be, however, that the intervention of the Secretary of State in the field of sixteen plus examinations already provides substantial evidence of the complex way in which DES thinking has been developing.

Commenting in 1983 on the criteria developed by the Joint Council of Examination Boards for the sixteen plus examinations in history, Sir Keith Joseph called for students to be helped towards an 'understanding of the intellectual, cultural, technological and political growth of the United Kingdom and of the effects of these developments on the lives of its citizens', reminding the Boards that, 'one of the aims of studying history is to understand the development of shared values which are a distinctive feature of British society and culture'. In this formulation, the general educational aims that students should have access to the most adequate information about the past that we have available and be encouraged to develop the skills necessary to understand different perspectives on what is known, appear to have become subsidiary to a need to assert *national* values.

There was immediate criticism. *The Times Educational Supplement*, 15 April 1983, commented sharply, 'his emphasis is quite plain: history cannot be seen simply as an opportunity to alert pupils 'to the possibility of bias . . . and to the risks of anachronism': history must also promote the national myths by which British people live'. His emphasis did indeed appear to suggest that the DES saw the world from a viewpoint which belonged more with Britain's imperial past than her interdependent present. Moreover, his comments were quite likely to be understood as a DES hint that examination syllabuses which give emphasis to world perspectives should in future be discouraged.

The Secretary of State, however, clarified his position at some length in an address to the Historical Association in February 1984, in which he argued that:

> values are shared only in a broad sense: we disagree among ourselves about much, and that is as it should be in an open society . . . but it is that commonality that defines us as a society. It is mercifully the case that almost all the people of this country subscribe, in general terms, to the value of liberty for the individual under the law, and believe that liberty is least insecure in a parliamentary democracy (*The Times Educational Supplement*, 17 February 1984).

This understanding of British institutions appears to be at the centre of his comments on the sixteen plus criteria and he shows some awareness of the contradiction inherent in the assertion of *British* values in a society which claims to value social, cultural and ethnic diversity. To handle this he attempts to make a clear distinction between 'an element of national history' and 'nationalistic history'. He is not specific as to what kinds of myths nationalist history would generate but he does attempt to pin down the inescapable parts of a school history course.

> British history has something to convey which cannot, however expert the teaching, be conveyed through Roman history or American history or Caribbean history.

> But throughout time, invasions and military conflicts, political, religious or economic movements, as well as exploration and migration, all serve to entwine a particular nation's story with those of other people with different origins and cultures. As time passes, as the dust of successive multiple changes settles, the nation constantly emerging from the crucible is more complex, and often enriched and revitalized; and the study of its history becomes correspondingly more complex and more subtle (ibid.).

What is most interesting about this exploration of the issues is the extent to which the disagreements and complexities are acknowledged and the belief in a 'correct' interpretation of history denied. 'There is a range of questions – be they political, economic, social or cultural – on which there is no single right answer' (ibid.). Thus while teachers of history are to avoid bias in selection, presentation and interpretation, it is fully accepted that this is very difficult to achieve and that teachers have to interpret the available evidence on the basis of their own personal set of values: 'variety in interpretation is not only legitimate – it is the stuff of history' (ibid.). Crucially, the teacher's job is to bring students to the point where they can begin to make their own interpretation (ibid.).

All of this clearly makes a valuable move onwards from earlier DES 'rhetoric' of 'instilling' values and 'providing' young people with values and standards.[3] It remains, however, to be seen whether the present prescription will, despite its recognition of the richness of Britain's cultural heritage, be able to avoid insularity by comparison with possible world perspectives. *Education for All* puts its contribution into the debate in these terms: 'a history syllabus which presents world history exclusively in terms of British interests, experiences and values could in no way be regarded as "sound" history' (DES, 1985).

Local Educational Authority Responses

The LEAs, as might be expected, do not present a consistent policy position on the appropriate curriculum for a multicultural society. As was indicated in the general discussion above, approaches range from those which see multicultural education as an add-on component to existing arrangements to those which propose a curriculum generated from the principles of equality and social justice. A growing number of LEAs now have publicly available policy documents but only a few of these are as far-reaching in their implications as those adopted by the Royal County of Berkshire and the ILEA.

It is, perhaps, valuable to consider what these two LEAs have to say about curriculum issues as their positions take the argument for change further than central government has yet been prepared to venture and they can be seen as offering an ideological challenge to those LEAs and schools who are reluctant even to begin the process of rethinking the curriculum.

Berkshire's *Education for Racial Equality* (Berkshire, 1983) sets out the values on which the policy is based, the programme of activities which are implied for teachers, the support to be provided, and the arrangements to be made for monitoring progress. The key curriculum question asked is: 'which topics in primary schools and which subjects and syllabuses in secondary schools are most relevant for developing understanding of racial equality and justice?' Teachers are challenged as to when and where in their schools pupils were likely to be learning, directly or indirectly, about concepts or themes such as: diversity, similarity, justice, civilisation, migration, racism, colonialism, resistance, interdependence.

A similar, though slightly less intellectually threatening approach is taken in the ILEA's *A Policy for Equality* (ILEA, 1983c,d,f) which has as one of its components an anti-racist statement together with a set of guidelines for practice. It is recognised in this document that there can be no one blueprint but rather a set of 'principles, directions and methods for development' (ILEA, 1983d). As with the Berkshire policy, ILEA teachers are challenged to sort out their own positions in relation to racism and culture and then to develop a curriculum guided by the following four principles:

(i) Very young children need both an affirmation of the value of people of all colours and cultures and to be helped towards avoidance of stereotypes and mis-representations which form at a very early age.

(ii) A wide range of content is important but it is essential that pupils develop analytical skills and can engage in an understanding of cross cultural perspectives and values.

(iii) Pupils and students must have opportunities to gain an historical perspective that is free from ethnocentric biases.

(iv) The whole curriculum must be open to all so that no sort of restricted access is given to some pupils because of stereotyped views of ability (ILEA, 1983d).

Examination Boards

Little and Willey (1981) stated that the examining boards in general reported that they 'saw no need systematically to review their syllabuses to consider their relevance to a multi-ethnic society'. Only one out of the eight GCE and fourteen CSE boards reported that it had conducted such a review. A number of CSE boards said that they were confident that the influence exerted by teachers would ensure that examinations reflected a multi-ethnic society to the extent to which teachers thought that they should, and drew attention to the opportunities afforded by Mode 3. Little and Willey recommended 'a systematic review of all existing syllabuses'.

A series of studies of individual subjects made for the Schools Council under the title *Assessment in a Multicultural Society* (Broadbent *et al.*, 1983; Fallows, 1983; File, 1983; Wood, 1984) reveals little progress from the positions described above. Noting this, *Education for All* (DES, 1985) proposes that the newly established Secondary Examination Council has an important role to play and suggests that, in particular, advice should be offered to the Secretary of State with respect to the new General Certificate of Secondary Education, and Certificate of Pre-Vocational Education, and Advanced Supplementary Levels. The view taken appears to be a pragmatic one that it is only the parts of the examination system which are subject to major upheavals that are susceptible to changes in perspective. Additionally, it may be necessary to argue that Swann does not go far enough and that changes at A-level and in university courses are of equal importance in bringing about any real changes in curriculum perspectives at school level.

School Responses

It is one of the most remarkable features of the UK educational system that change can be set in motion in individual schools without having to wait for external directives from DES or LEAs, and that even in relation to examinations, it is possible, by means of the Mode 3 model of assessment, for individual schools to determine the content and concepts to be assessed. It is in the hands of individual schools to respond to requests by students and parents for 'community' languages to be offered as examination subjects. Similarly schools have a relatively free hand to develop syllabuses in, for example, World Studies or Peace Studies if the staff think that these perspectives will be of benefit to the students in their care.

This freedom is accompanied by responsibilities to test out changes that are proposed against the best knowledge available, and to listen to the views of students, parents, governors and others closely involved in the community. An example of this can be seen where concern both to counter the racism experienced by black students and to deter any young people from joining white racist groups has led parents, teachers and other interested people to come together to discuss the ways in which schools can contribute to tackling racism. Some primary and secondary schools have, on this basis, developed policies for tackling racism which have made explicit to all concerned, teachers, students and parents, the value system from which the school is operating. An example of such a policy may suggest the nature of the discussions in one school and its possible outcomes in terms of its implications for the curriculum.

The curriculum can be a potent force for perpetuating racism. A prime cause of prejudice is ignorance and misunderstanding. If the curriculum has an ethnocentric perspective, it can lead to distortion, omission and misrepresentation of the historical and cultural experience of peoples. The curriculum, explicit and hidden, must aim, through overarching whole-school policies, the separate subject department syllabuses, the tutorial programme, and all curriculum planning:

(i)   to create an understanding of and interest in different environments, societies, systems and cultures across the world.

(ii) to study the political, social and economic reasons for racism and inequality, and their present-day effects in this country and the world.

(iii) to encourage pupils to recognise that each society has its own values, traditions and everyday living patterns which should be considered in the context of that society.

(iv) to study scientific achievements outside the western world, and alternative approaches to science.

(v)   to explore and share the ideas, opinions and interests which derive from particular cultural experience. Its content should be so selected that it engages pupils' feeling as well as giving them skills and information.

(vi) to develop the concepts and skills which will allow pupils to criticise and actively participate in all social institutions, e.g. media, political parties, etc.[4]

Planning the Curriculum

The remainder of this chapter concentrates on the issues involved in planning and enactment of the curriculum in the school, discussing first the realisation of a school's aims in the timetable and the choices to be made in relation to content and organisation of courses. This is followed by a discussion of what is involved in terms of the interaction between teacher and student.

As the school timetable represents the school's strategy for translating its aims into practice, inspection of what the timetable makes possible – or prevents – can reveal the seriousness with which generally agreed aims are taken. Schools which have become aware of a relationship between some groupings of options at fourth-year secondary level and low aspirations on the part of some students will, it seems likely, wish to ensure that the broad outlines of timetable arrangements do not function as a means of limiting the career possibilities of certain groups of students, even though the consequence of keeping them within a mainstream pattern of option choice may be a re-thinking of how those mainstream subjects are taught. The decisions represented in the timetable can also reveal either an important emphasis on or, alternatively, a disregard for the first languages of some students. A secondary school which decides to think through the implications of 'modern languages' such as Gujerati, Polish and Greek being available to students only after school or on Saturday mornings (perhaps on the same school premises) is likely to undertake a review of its languages policy and in a few schools first languages other than English are now being made available to examination classes alongside, or instead of, the European languages traditionally offered. A further development within this context is the rearrangement of early secondary language courses so that students are introduced to a range of languages and cultures before making option choices.[5] In scrutinising the timetable, it may also be significant to see whether the timetable arrangements act to separate out, or to keep in the mainstream of the curriculum, those students who need support in becoming fully bilingual.

The timetable, important as the structures it creates may be, is, however, only the first level of realisation of the school's intentions. The main burden of translating aims into planned content and appropriate pedagogies falls on individuals or groups of teachers and, whether the planning is being done by a single teacher for one primary class or by an inter-disciplinary team for a group of secondary classes, decisions have to be made about emphasis. Thus teachers usually find themselves following one of the two possible approaches which can for convenience be referred to respectively as 'permeation' and 'special emphasis'.

The 'permeation' approach is that discussed in relation to multicultural education above. Within it, the dimensions of race, class and gender are all subsumed with the generally agreed aim that students should be enabled to acquire the skills, knowledge and attributes appropriate for living and working in a specific and changing society, aware of its history, its present nature, and conflicting views on its future development. This provides the focus and the agenda for those planning courses. Content and pedagogy are decided on the basis of a series of questions as to what view of the world is being conveyed to students. It involves an active seeking out of alternative explanations and perspectives: seeing the world as others see it. In this approach, there are few elements specially identifiable as 'multicultural', 'anti-racist' or 'gender/class related'. These elements are taken for granted as dimensions which will be made visible in *all* that students study or take part in.

The alternative approach argues that although education for a multicultural society, or education for equality and social justice, should be the organising principle in planning courses, there is a need for there to be *specially visible* recognition of key issues and some in-depth study undertaken. It also sees school as one of several sites of struggle for alternative definitions and perspectives and argues that the taken-for-granted, dominant ideology can only be tackled by giving sufficient space and emphasis to alternative positions.

The kind of work implied by such an approach can be seen in the historical investigations which led to the publication of *Black Settlers in Britain 1555–1958* (File and Power, 1981). A further example can be found in the use made of the CEE English depth study options to look at language use or to read an author (or authors) of the student's own choice. Such studies in different subjects offer opportunities for students and teachers alike to encounter and analyse history, language issues, and cultural perspectives for which there might otherwise be no available space.

Both of the approaches outlined depend on *visibility* for the effectiveness of their operation. In the case of the *permeation* approach, its effectiveness relies on the issues being visible in all appropriate contexts. If the visibility which is claimed by those creating and teaching the courses is not achieved, the general statement of the aim of preparing students for living in a specific and changing society will not be adequately realised either.

In the case of the special *emphasis* approach, visibility is assured. The dangers are, first, that it tends to take the pressure off other teachers to examine their assumptions and content, and second, that a separation can develop between special studies and mainstream courses, with the special studies being seen as of relevance only to particular groups of students.

In practice, the two approaches are interdependent. Teachers need space in which to explore the relation between different historical, linguistic, social and cultural perspectives in order to be able to achieve the shifts in thinking which the *permeation* approach requires. In this, joint explorations with the students may have possibilities which could not be achieved by the teacher on his or her own. Take, for example, a teacher of French or German who finds time to discuss with his or her students the accents, dialects, or creoles which they have in their personal repertoires. This can open up possibilities for examining the relationship of the standard forms of French and German to dialect and creole forms in those languages, and lead into discussion of attitudes to language use. A comparable investigation in science might be focused on the history and cultural bias of a particular area of scientific discovery or technological application of science. (See Mears below.) Such joint investigations appear to be of considerable value in keeping the creativity of students and teachers alive. It is when teachers share their intellectual curiosity with their students, and when teacher and student share a continuing interest in each other's world picture, that the perspectives of both can become fully developed.

Classroom Negotiation of the Curriculum

It is perhaps useful at this point to revisit Jenkins and Shipman's 'trading post' image of the curriculum. For them, the curriculum is essentially the enacted or *experienced* curriculum. The curriculum is made in the classroom through the negotiations and transactions which take place there in the context of the school seen as, 'a socialising institution charged by society with the task of handing on to pupils something of society's intellectual, emotional and technical capital' (Jenkins and Shipman, 1976). Their image suggests that in schools the students not only have something to trade, that they do not come empty-handed, rather, as has been argued here, bearing a rich accumulation of experience, language, cultural awareness and historical and political understanding, but also that they can be *denied* access to society's material and cultural 'capital' as a result of what takes place in the classroom.

James has written, with a light touch of irony, that all students should 'know their place' adding that if you really *do* know your place you know and understand 'how it comes to be and how it might be otherwise' (James, 1979). In this, he is putting forward a very similar view to that of Hall who in discussing how racism might be approached by teachers of social studies, suggests that the main task in the classroom is to 'deconstruct the obvious'.

One has to show that there are social and historical processes and that they are not written in the stars, they are not handed down. They are deep conditions which are not going to change if we start tinkering around with them. We must not give our students that kind of illusion. We can however begin the process of questioning what the structures are and how they work (Hall, 1979).

Such questioning of 'what the structures are and how they work' implies a pedagogy which enables students to gain access for themselves to as accurate information about the world as is available and to be encouraged to develop the skill in interpretation necessary to be able to handle the material available intelligently. In this respect, much lies with the power of the teacher in the classroom; either to make available the channels to the range of explanation and interpretation available in the adult world, complete with anomalies and contradictions, or to leave them blocked by ignorance or lack of skill in handling ideas.

This raises perhaps the most important discussion of all for, if the curriculum is to be opened up in terms of breadth of perspective and its ability to challenge such deep-seated conditions as racism and sexism for *all* students, the levels of expectation which we have hitherto maintained in relation to age and 'ability' have to be reconsidered and additional ways of perceiving them opened up also. A major re-examination or re-forming of existing curricula makes possible a parallel raising of existing levels of expectation of what all students can achieve. A strong form of this argument sees in mixed ability grouping and styles of teaching the only means by which such ends can be achieved. A weaker form suggests that the key location for such re-examination of levels of expectation would be in the minute-by-minute transactions of knowledge, in the individual skills developed and in confidence built or destroyed. This has to be set against an understanding of the ways in which engagement with students can be blighted by the pressures exerted by the institutional setting or by the experiences of society which they bring with them to school.

A whole series of pedagogical strategies for the development of students' powers in reading, writing and discussion are needed if the pedagogy is to match the decisions which have to be made about the content of the curriculum. Donaldson has pushed back our preconceptions about the ages at which the young child may be capable of recognising intentions in others and hence appreciate the relativity of his or her own view, suggesting that, 'the normal child comes to school with well-established skills as a thinker' and attacking those in charge of education for their failure to enable their students, 'to make sense of the world and bring it under deliberate control' (Donaldson, 1978), and the study by Burgess below suggests the ways in which the examination of content can go hand in hand with new expectations of what young children can do.

The equivalent evaluation of what can be expected of the vast majority of secondary students has yet to be fully undertaken, but there are important reasons why this should be seen as a high priority. Black parents' demands that schools shall expect more from their children, and the critique of mainstream education which is implied in the work of the supplementary schools can only be answered by schools setting a high value on encouraging the full cognitive and affective development of *all* their students. Secondly, if priority is given to the aim of enabling students to think for themselves and take on responsibilities in society, a new emphasis will be needed on extending, across the ability range, our expectation of who can become confident as thinkers including a confidence to test out their ideas for internal consistency and truth to the world as they know it. Students of all backgrounds and in all kinds of schools who are encouraged to read widely and critically, who discuss and work together and are enabled to develop a sense of power in their ability to express themselves in speech and writing, may well come to have exactly the qualities needed to become actively anti-racist or anti-sexist, or more generally in the words of the Warnock Report to become, 'an active participant in society and a responsible contributor to it' (DES, 1978b). Students who are not encouraged in this way are likely to become neither active nor responsible.

This line of argument has a sting in the tail for there are both possibilities and contradictions inherent in such a set of priorities. Students who have developed a critical intelligence and have been encouraged to *participate actively* in society may well look very critically at the processes by which they may be denied employment or are having their life chances limited in various ways. Young people, as Grace points out, who have developed a critical intelligence through their education and who go out into a world where that form of critical intelligence seems to open up no opportunities whatsoever are, 'a growing contradiction in our social arrangements' (Grace, 1980).

Towards a Dynamic Curriculum

The Parliamentary Select Committee on Education, Science and Arts, suggests in its Second Report that a school's curriculum should be seen as a 'contract' taking the form of published statement of curricular aims: This, it suggests, would represent a consensus in which individual schools and their governing bodies would play a major part. 'The responsibility would be a shared one with the fullest possible involvement of teacher, parents, employers, local community, and local education authority' (Select Committee on Education, Science and the Arts, 1982).

The omission of the DES reflects the Select Committee's disenchantment with central government's contribution to the curriculum debate. In its model, responsibility for breadth lies with the LEA through its officers and advisers, but the onus for getting a curriculum which meets the needs of society ultimately lies with the school: 'The public statement would be the basis for a regular process of self-assessment by the school which we believe would generate a dynamic rather than a static curriculum' (DES, 1982). The Select Committee's model may have a number of difficulties inherent within it – the need to balance local imperatives and parochialism against wider concerns may be one of the foremost. On the other hand, it faces up to the problem involved in framing a curriculum for a multicultural, changing society by recognising that the curriculum itself has to be continually evolving and to find practical ways of holding in balance conflicting views, values and interests.

It has been the argument of this chapter that, at any moment, the curriculum involves all the factors which make up the DES, LEA, examination board, school and classroom arrangements which influence the selection of one item of knowledge rather than another and that, most importantly, the curriculum is negotiated in classroom conversations between students and teachers, with individual teachers bearing a major responsibility for whether students' capabilities are extended or limited. Changes can be brought about on all these levels; perspectives and priorities can be changed and new practices developed. The important issue in this continual re-making of the curriculum is whether it functions to highlight and analyse the underlying inequalities which are such crucial features of contemporary life, or whether its construction ensures that such uncomfortable contradictions are suppressed.

Our success in facing up to the difficulties that have to be tackled will show very clearly in the school curriculum. It makes visible the response that society makes to its diversity either by creating space and giving recognition or by resisting any incursions. It also makes visible, since the curriculum is, theoretically, based on principled choices, the value systems of the society at large. It shows up how far there is real interest in enabling students to develop 'lively enquiring minds'. It reveals the ambiguities of what is meant by the 'instilling' of 'respect for religious and moral values' and 'tolerance [sic] of other races, religions and ways of life'. Crucially, it exposes whether the stated intentions of helping students 'to understand the world in which they live' (DES, 1981b) extends to *all* the facts – including the uncomfortable ones.

NOTES

1   See for example:
National Union of Teachers (1978) *All our Children.* London: NUT.
BOLTON, E. (1979) in *Trends in Education* 4. London: HMSO.
Department of Education and Science (1985) *Education for All, The Report of the Committee of Inquiry into the Education of Children from Ethnic Minority Groups* (Swann Report). London: HMSO.

2   Some examples:
Redbridge CRC (1978) *Cause for Concern.*
OWAAD (1980) *Black Women in Britain Speak Out.*
DHONDY, F. (1978) 'Teaching Young Blacks', *Race Today*, May/June. London: Race Today Collective.
CARBY, H. (1980) 'Multiculture', *Screen Education* 34. London: Society for Education in Film and Television.
MULLARD, C. (1981) *Racism in Society and Schools: History, Policy, Practice.* Centre for Multicultural Education Occasional Paper 1, University of London Institute of Education.

3   Speech by Under-Secretary of State for Education, Rt. Hon. Rhodes Boyson, MP, to Conservative Party in Loughborough 5 February 1982. Source, Conservative Party Central Office Press Release.
See also Department of Education and Science (1981) *The School Curriculum.* London: HMSO.

4 North Westminster Community School: 'Towards a Multicultural Philosophy'. See also the Interim Statement of Policy by the Staff and Governors (1980) 'The Idea of a Community School'.
5 One of the consequences of the policy re-thinking referred to in note 4 has been the re-writing of modern language courses at North Westminster Community School.

7 Curriculum Considerations in the Primary School

Tom Vassen

Multicultural education is often understood by white teachers as something that only black children are in need of, or yet another passing innovation. I am of the view that what is needed is a full review of the curriculum to consider its relevance to a multicultural society.

> What is needed is that sensitive consideration should be given to such matters as the extent to which and the way in which materials accurately and fairly depict members of minority groups and reflect their position in British society (Willey, 1982b).

Britain is a complex society comprising a number of cultures whose origins can easily be identified with the country's colonial past, and many of the political and economic problems that are present in our society and indeed in the world community arise out of Britain's international connections. Yet there is little evidence to suggest that our teaching takes into account this phenomenon. For example, an honest and objective examination and analysis of immigration to this country in particular, and migration in general, might go a long way to eliminate painful remarks like, 'Get back to your country!' There has been a consistent failure to recognise that black British people form part of this society.

The ethnocentricism of our curriculum actually generates and promotes racial antagonism. If 'what we transmit in the process of schooling reflects culture' (Lawton, 1980), then syllabus provision in schools is obviously lop-sided. As David Hicks says, 'The dangers of [an Anglocentric curriculum] are manifest in its transmission of biased views and the belittling – often through omission – often unwilling – of prejudice and racist attitudes' (Hicks, 1981).

Apologists will contend that racism is a minor irritant in people's lives; that it is overplayed by the hypersensitive; that sheer will and application will neutralise its so called damaging effects. Yet racism degrades, deprives and causes minorities to exist on the fringes of mainstream society. This view, born of experience, coincides with the official Rampton Committee view which concluded that though racism, whether intentional or unintentional, cannot be said alone to account for the underachievement of West Indian children, it can and does have an important bearing on their performance at school (DES, 1981a).

A multicultural curriculum on the other hand, is one that recognises the validity of all cultures and ought not, in my view, to be interpreted as a compensatory model or a strategy to arrest and control black resistance. To be sure, it is precisely the anger and resistance of minorities that has secured a change in attitude of education authorities up and down the country. The ILEA for instance, has made it incumbent upon all its schools to submit a policy statement that takes into account fair and equal provision for all its pupils (ILEA, 1983b). This is discussed further in Chapters 5 and 6. In a similar fashion, some of the teachers' unions have taken seriously the issue of racism and education. A document by the NUT (1982) claimed:

> The development of a multicultural curriculum and awareness is not a minority issue: it is by widening the horizons of the majority of our pupils that they will be prepared for life in a multicultural, multiracial Britain, and racial harmony will not be achieved without increasing the level of intellectual understanding awareness and respect among our own pupils (NUT, 1982).

In the not so recent past, it was the pious belief that attitude change almost alone would nullify the racism inherent in our curriculum. Latterly educationists and teachers are calling for a complete reappraisal of what we transmit to our pupils through their lessons. Obviously, both are prerequisites for an equal and fair education.

Curriculum Development in Four Primary Schools

It was in an attempt to clarify the issues involved in changing a school's curriculum to enable it to meet more adequately the needs of all children, that four primary schools in London were studied in some detail. The investigation was an attempt to identify areas where support was needed if effective change were to occur, and also to highlight instances where schools had changed, and the processes which had facilitated such changes. Below I suggest a preliminary checklist for curriculum development, based on the findings of this work.

(i) Do materials and displays in the classroom and school as a whole relate to Britain as a multicultural society?

(ii) Is there a diversity of cultures represented in all aspects of learning?

(iii) Are teaching materials, e.g. dressing up corners, wall charts, games, dolls, jig-saw puzzles, mathematics and reading schemes, so constructed or selected that they represent all groups?

(iv) Do staff meetings consider bias in learning materials?

(v) Are negative or stereotyped images in learning materials discussed by staff and teachers and class?

(vi) Is the school assembly doctrinaire in its approach?

(vii) Does the school support and encourage the children's need to adhere to their cultural traditions?

(viii) Does the provision of school meals take into account cultural or religious customs?

(ix) Has the school discussed the cultural bias in testing?

(x) Do children work in mixed ability and sex groups and is collaborative work encouraged?

(xi) Is there adequate provision for second language learners?

(xii) Are dialect and mother tongue recognised?

(xiii) Are disciplinary problems merely considered in terms of blackness or are all social considerations taken into account?

(xiv) What links exist between the school and home?

(xv) Does the school encourage home visits?

(xvi) Is there a postholder for multicultural education?

(xvii) What consideration is given to professional development?

Unless children are consciously brought up in an atmosphere where racism and prejudice are natural to them, they tend to relate to each other, irrespective of race, colour and creed, quite spontaneously with few reservations. Where this harmonious interaction does not exist (and it does not in many primary schools) the discerning teacher can and should engineer situations that will ensure this ethos. Interesting, exciting and gainful experiences, I find, work exceedingly well across both race and sex lines. These include the following:

(i) Primary school classrooms usually have 'dressing-up corners/boxes'. These can be used with very successful results if they contain items of dress representing a number of national traditional costumes.

(ii) The interest table can be employed positively by including objects and artefacts from various backgrounds.

(iii) Stories and folk tales from many cultures can be told.

(iv) Arts and crafts provide a number of possibilities – masks, dolls, calligraphy, painting, designs and patterns.

(v) Music that represents all traditions can demonstrate the diversity and similarity between cultures.

(vi) Visits to local street markets reveal the impact that minorities have had on British society.

(vii) Cooking and the tasting of different foods can and does break down irrational fears and prejudice.

(viii) School educational excursions to museums and exhibitions where ethnic interests are regular features can be valuable.

(ix) Children of various cultural backgrounds are perhaps the most valuable resource – they can demonstrate and explain reasons for traditional clothing and eating preferences. They can also demonstrate and teach English-speaking children their own script.

Second-language learners can be a remarkable resource in giving others an awareness of the difficulties of learning a second language, e.g. a Bangladeshi child appeared to be learning extremely slowly. When I provided her with stories in her own language and the equivalent English translation her learning took off with amazing acceleration. Furthermore her peers developed an instantaneous respect for her literacy. The classroom now abounds with signs and notices in Bangla (written by her) and English. Moreover the English-speaking children have developed a very keen interest in Bangla script and many of them are attempting to write simple sentences and their names in it. The frightened, timid child who entered school is now confident and assertive. The children have discovered that she has something to offer. Also, there is now amongst one class at least, a direct awareness of the difficulties of the second-language learner.

The consensus among the teachers in these four inner London schools was that, though they attempted to include in their teaching 'multicultural elements' that would demonstrate a multicultural curriculum, they were handicapped by their lack of knowledge about the diversity of cultures represented in their schools; their inability to define multicultural education; and a lack of teaching resources. Heads and staff observed that while there is an abundance of materials and resources in their schools that deal with European cultures, there is very little on Asian, Irish, West Indian and African. Where there are materials that deal with the latter, they are often contemptuous, patronising, distorted and casual. The attitude to African history, for instance, may well be due to people like Professor Hugh Trevor Roper who has stated:

Perhaps in the future there will be some African history to teach but at present there is none, or very little: there is only the history of Europeans in Africa, the rest is largely darkness . . . and darkness is not a subject for history. (quoted in Twitchin and Demuth, 1981).

There was the very strong feeling of genuine outrage among the majority of teachers that the whole subject of colonialism and slavery is less than accurately and honestly dealt with. Younger teachers of between three to five years' teaching experience were highly critical of their initial teacher training which took very little or no account of the reality of a multicultural society. Many indeed felt ill-prepared upon taking up the first appointments. Now that a few have had the benefit of in-service training in the area, there was some degree of confidence in taking on new ideas. There was the view that a few teachers by themselves cannot adequately influence the whole school. What some were in effect arguing for was on site in-service training much along the lines of the ILEA Lambeth Whole School Project. The initiatives, it seems, would have to come from heads, inspectors, advisory teachers or the local authority.

All schools stated that they had some information on the subject. Their materials were accessible to all staff. They were in the main NUT booklets, local authority documents and publications – valid, relevant and invaluable guides but nowhere near enough adequate to inform staff in the area.

In one respect all four heads were consistent and positive. This was in their unequivocal opposition to any form of overt racism within the school. The contradiction, however, was that the bookshelves abounded with materials that were offensive, although it would only be fair to state that the staff are in the process of checking for these materials. The task is laborious as they felt there was no structured way of looking at the whole area of race. Consequently, in general, much of the work was piecemeal.

Community links were regarded by staff and heads as crucial if there were to be any coherent approach to all the issues. Parent-Teacher Associations, though small, met regularly and have been informed of the schools' commitment to a multicultural and anti-racist approach.

The lesson that can be drawn from this admittedly limited study can only be regarded as indicative. What does emerge is that there is a need for a more considered strategy of in-service training and other interventions. The remainder of this chapter discusses these issues in more detail, namely in-service training, with particular reference to whole school policies, local authority support and school/community links.

In-Service Training

The development of multicultural education is characterised by urgent, new requirements. The changes are fundamentally twofold. First, children are going to be prepared for a hoped-for new society; second, the nature of the school is going to undergo change in terms of organisation, administration and policy.

Teachers are going to have to address themselves to the task of responding to a wide range of change, which will entail not only the re-evaluation of the curriculum but, very importantly, the willingness to re-orientate attitudes. As the Brent Committee Report points out, 'In fact the changes in content and materials are really the reflections of much more significant changes in attitudes' (Report 44/182 Brent Education Committee, 1982).

Both the Scarman Report (Home Office, 1981) and the

Rampton Report (DES, 1981a) strongly support and recommend in-service training in multicultural education. 'The committee attaches considerable importance to the development of in-service education as the most effective means of directly affecting teachers in our schools in the immediate future' (DES, 1981a). Of most importance in this area are awareness and attitudes. No matter how liberal and emancipated teachers as a group may see themselves, racism in its unintentional form persists. The conditioning has been deep rooted and almost indelible.

As a set of routine practices and relationships, racism is frequently invisible to white people. As a set of beliefs and attitudes it is frequently unconscious. In neither of these two aspects, therefore, is it considered by most people to be a serious problem. On the contrary most people dismiss the view that Britain is a racist society (Berkshire Local Education Authority, 1982).

A well-structured, carefully considered, in-service training programme should be a permanent feature in all LEAs. To meet these new needs, a body of well-trained, experienced and qualified staff should be constituted to work closely with the inspectors, advisory teachers, heads and staffs.

From the four-school study just described it would appear that courses would need to fulfil essential background issues to take account of the following:

  (i) Race and racism.
 (ii) Historical reasons for migration – the evolution of capitalism and imperialism.
(iii) The experience of minorities and their marginalisation.
 (iv) Attitudes to minorities.
  (v) Curriculum development.
 (vi) Exploring strategies for making links with the community.
(vii) Information and skills in dealing with parents and children sensitively.

However, the skills, strategies and information gathered by teachers on such in-service courses are generally not disseminated to their respective staffs. One other disadvantage is that this in-service material is received second-hand and the recipient staffs do not actually participate to the desired level.

Further, there is a justifiable belief that in-service training courses held after school hours usually attract the self-motivated teachers. As multicultural education is aimed at the school in its entirety, it is reasonable to expect that in-service training should reach all staff in any one school. However, it would be unreasonable, impractical and unrealistic to expect whole staffs to attend courses of any description, especially those during school hours.

It is initiatives like the ILEA's Lambeth Whole School Project that have the greatest chance of success in the development of teachers simply because the work is conducted on site where strategies can actually be tested in classrooms. There is also the advantage of in-service education reaching whole staffs of any one school. The results will or should be continuity, coherence and, in some cases, subtle pressure on resistant teachers. The monumental task undertaken by the Project was made even more onerous by the team's policy of adopting a low profile in order to make it appear that initiatives came from the teachers themselves. Unfortunately what most staff really expected was a cut-and- dried presentation of a multicultural education curriculum amply laced with thirty to forty lessons that would cover a year's work. In this respect staff expectations were not fulfilled, and rightly so.

Despite initial reactions of staff that did not augur well for the project, the work has had enduring and positive effects.

> It may well be that lasting change can best be created by the means the team are using. They have certainly made progress and it is evident that in-school projects are capable of responding to the special needs of a school beyond those of voluntary recruited courses (Eggleston, Dunn, Purewal, 1981).

Space prevents the giving of a comprehensive picture of the work done by the Lambeth Whole School Project. Of the six schools selected to work within the framework of the Project only three stayed the distance. This reveals a commitment by those three at least to attempt change. Of those which did not, it can be best explained by the statement of a head who left the project when she asked, 'What happens when the project comes to an end?' I offer here a summary only of the positive and lasting effects of the work the team has had on one school.

(i) The school now sees itself as a multicultural school and states this in its brochure.

(ii) Every culture present in the school is valued and recognised in curriculum planning.

(iii) The school possesses a great variety of multicultural resources.

(iv) School assemblies are consciously non-doctrinaire.

(v) The library has undergone significant changes as books are closely examined for offensive texts and images.

(vi) Parents, for the first time in the school's history, accompany children on excursions.

(vii) Conferences have been held to examine every implication race has for the school.

(viii) The school steelband has participated in festivals and undertaken a tour of Devon primary schools.

(ix) A book exhibition and food fair was held for parents.

(x) A post of responsibility for multicultural education has been created.

(xi) A parents' workshop has been established.

(xii) The school has participated in the Caribbean teacher exchange programme.

(xiii) There is a greater awareness of social problems and issues which the school as a whole, for the first time, is considering in terms of understanding children. Very importantly problems of a social nature are seen in terms of class rather than colour.

(xiv) The school is at present conducting its own in-service training which is considering the reassessment and development of the whole curriculum.

Local Education Authority Support

Jones and Kimberley note the 'extreme reluctance of some LEAs and schools across the country to respond to even the mild DES exhortations that the curriculum for all students should reflect the multiethnic nature of society at large' (Jones and Kimberley, 1982). In this observation the key word may well be 'mild'. That LEAs have not responded positively may in part be due to the fact that the DES, the highest education body in the land, has not been direct, decisive and authoritative in its pronouncements.

To its credit the ILEA's response has been exemplary. Yet it was not without pressure from practising and committed teachers, interest groups like NAME, ALTARF and CTA, and community pressure groups.

The ILEA's initial attention focused on four major areas:

(i) Gathering information and statistics on minorities so that policies could be formulated.
(ii) Supporting work that encouraged equal education.
(iii) Establishing links with local ethnic communities.
(iv) Supporting positive discrimination.

The effects of these initiatives yielded positive results. The gathering of statistics, although highly controversial, revealed the compelling need to make greater provision for second-language learners. It also uncovered the over-representation of West Indian children in 'sin' bins. Support work received a boost in the establishment of a multi-ethnic inspectorate. In addition, the Lambeth Whole School Project discussed above, and the East London Whole School Project, following on action research work done during the Schools Council/NFER Education for a Multicultural Society Project, were set up to promote school based, school focused in-service education. Subsequently ILEA policy, described in more detail in Chapter 2, built on and made more specific the authority's goals in relation to multi-ethnic education.

While the ILEA figures very prominently in this section, it must be realised that other authorities such as Berkshire, Brent, Haringey and Coventry have also gone a long way to meet the challenge in contemporary education.

LEA policies by themselves are not enough, nor are they intended to be. What is also needed, as the more recent ILEA policies stipulate, is an individual school policy. The school has a major part to play in the development of a harmonious multicultural society for it is at least the one area which children have in common. There is, therefore, the need for all schools to inform parents that the school policy is committed to an equal education in accordance with DES Circulars 14/77 and 15/78.

Such a policy must assure all students and parents that:

(i) all children are regarded as being of equal value;
(ii) the school will foster harmonious relations between all sections and both sexes of the community;
(iii) all children have the inalienable right to be educated for life in a multicultural society;

(iv) the school includes in its broad aims the inculcation of self-respect and respect for others.

Finally, such a policy must:

in the day to day running of the school . . . demonstrate to all those associated with the school that our aims are important to us as an institution. All staff must be vigilant in seeing that no unacceptable racist behaviour, from whatever source, is tolerated (NUT, 1982).

The importance of parental involvement cannot be stressed sufficiently and to give it credibility it should be concerned with the formulation of general policy that will affect the day-to-day running of the school. The policy would then be seen to have greater relevance for the local community for parents are usually more in touch with the neighbourhood and its particular needs.

Parental Consultation and Involvement

When schools reap a rich harvest of achievement which they have not sown and only in part have nurtured, they will too eagerly accept the kudos. When the crop is 'blighted', the failure is so easily ascribed to the home of which teachers have very scant knowledge.

The schooling of children is a tacit partnership between parents and teachers. But many parents are now beginning to view the school as the sleeping partner. The myth that black parents in particular are unconcerned is exploded by the growth of supplementary schools, the opposition to bussing in the sixties and to questioning of the disproportionate placement of their children in ESN schools.

Lack of involvement has three main strands. First, the unwillingness of teachers to participate with parents who are regarded as 'non-professionals' and thereby not qualified to offer anything. Second, the notion that parents' duties cease at the school gate. Third, the schools' rigidity in structuring visits which do not take into account the work commitments of parents.

If there is to be meaningful understanding of children's backgrounds then the brief encounters of the open evening and annual concert are not going to fulfil this need. 'Only if parents and schools can be brought closer together will parents appreciate what schools are trying to do for their children and teachers understand the parents' expectations' (Home Office, 1981).

The following is a list of some strategies that could be adopted by schools to form close links with parents:

  (i) establishing a Parents, Teachers and Friends Association;
 (ii) social functions where parents, teachers and interested parties can mix on an informal basis;
(iii) organising events which encourage various cultural interests;
 (iv) parents' evenings planned with flexibility and consultation;
  (v) parents with expertise in various skills can be encouraged to work with teachers in classrooms. Cookery, woodwork, art and craft offer suitable opportunities;
 (vi) parents talking to children about their occupations and for background diversity (religion, traditions, customs);
(vii) establishing a parents' room with library containing examples of children's work as well as reading for adults.

Finally, as one LEA pointed out:

> Teachers must be aware of varying parental attitudes to school and their concept of school. Schools are thought to have very different functions by different cultural groups. Schools must be aware of this and ensure that parents feel they are welcome in schools and are participants in the educational process (Brent Education Committee in conjunction with Brent Teachers' Association (NUT), 1980).

Many primary schools have a long way to go before they adequately meet the needs of all their children, both black and white. This chapter has attempted to demonstrate that progress is possible but that it requires a considerable amount of co-ordinated work by all involved – not just teachers – if effective progress is to be made.

8 Tackling Racism and Sexism in the Primary Classroom

Celia Burgess

Girl: 'The children in the nursery, those pictures on the wall are just full of white children and when they've only got little minds, in their minds they might think the world is mostly full of white people . . . '

Boy: ' . . . and say if an Indian child was looking at a book with only white people in he would think that his sort of colour ain't important in the school.'

(From a discussion with junior school children about their infant readers.)

Girl: When we looked at the books in school we saw nearly all boys playing games. All we saw of the girls' games were things like skipping and playing with dolls.'

Teacher: What do you think you would like to say to the people who make all the books we looked at?'

Girl: 'We're angry about it. We're angry. We'd all like to say, can you make a book that's all about girls – playing all the things that the boys do?'

(Second year junior girls discussing books they read and one they have made themselves.)

Schools, like all institutions in our society, are both racist and sexist in their power structures; in the processes by which they assess and divide children; in the attitudes and expectations of some teachers; in their curricula; and in the all-pervasive hidden curriculum in which children are immersed. The children quoted above already have experienced something of the impact of the racist and sexist stereotyping which surrounds them in their daily lives and, crucially, in school. From their account, racist and sexist messages have been present in the curriculum from the beginning of their attendance at school. Much must be done, of course, if those children at a later stage are not to be expressing their criticisms of the ways in which selection procedures and teacher expectations have severely restricted what is possible to them in terms of educational outcomes as girls or black children. It seems clear, however, that one of the aims of anti-sexist, anti-racist teaching must be to challenge the curriculum, materials and resources for their bias, and to attempt to have input that gives more than tokenistic recognition to the experience and contribution of women and black people to society, both past and present; and to develop materials that do not contain gross stereotypes, glaring omissions and serious distortions. Children, like those quoted above, who have begun to question the images they find around them and who are alert to the need to challenge statements which are taken for granted, cannot be said to have acquired a full range of techniques for detecting ideological processes at work – but they have *started* to do just that. Their own experience provides them with many powerful starting points of which teachers can take advantage. They can be helped to articulate and test out their unease or anger at what they see to be unfair. It can be argued that it is very important that they should learn to evaluate critically: material, images, statements and ideas. These are the intellectual and political skills necessary for understanding and acting in the world.

They can also learn that ideas are not just free floating but are connected to who has power. 'Who is writing what and for whom?' – the title of an article by Petronella Breinburg (1980) – is a question that primary-age children are capable of answering, as in the following discussion:

> *Teacher*: 'Why do you think most of the reading books only show white people?'
>
> *Girl*: 'Because it's the white people who publish them. There's not many black people publish books. If it was lots of black people did publish books there would be lots of black people in them and if a Indian person was to write a book or publish a book *they* would put an Indian child in the story. But mostly because it's the white people who publish books . . . and they don't think of other countries, except their own colour.'
>
> *Boy*: 'I know why, sir. It's because the white people who print the books, they think that white people should be higher than black people – that's why they put them in the books and pictures.'
>
> (black nine and ten year olds)

In the primary classroom, the study of racism and sexism in the curriculum does not have to be an abstract intellectual exercise as it can constantly be tied into children's own experience:

> 'I read this book called *Charlie and the Chocolate Factory* and in it there were these sort of imp people who worked for the man in the factory and they were sort of like coloured people – all their hair was sticking out and they weren't wearing any tops and were wearing grass skirts and they had bare feet and sang funny songs.'

Teacher: 'Why didn't you like this?'

> 'I never liked them because when other children read it if they're not a coloured person they might sort of take the mickey out of them out of that book and get the idea that coloured people run around in grass skirts in other countries.'

And from a discussion on why so many books show boys riding bikes and very few girls:

Teacher: 'Is that why there are more pictures – because girls don't really like riding?'

Boy: 'I don't think they like to race and all that sort of thing.'

Boy: 'And there was ninety-nine boys and thirty-nine girls in my books. Girls go down and boys go up.'

Teacher: 'OK let's see what the girls think. He said it was because girls don't like riding bikes.'

Girl: 'Because girls keep falling off.'

Teacher: 'Do you like riding a bike?'

Girl: 'Yes.'

Teacher: 'Do you keep falling off?'

Girl: 'No. But when I was young and I stay out with my sister people keep *pushing me off.* That's why I don't ride my bike now.'

Teacher: 'What people?'

Girl: 'These two boys who used to live up the road.'

In the following excerpt from a discussion about Harriet Tubman[1] not only are the children relating what they have learned to what they know of the present, they are beginning to explore the nature of history itself, especially what counts as evidence and who controls its availability.

Boy: 'We should have half of each so we could have white and black people's history together. I think if white people study it they might not be so prejudice.'

Teacher: 'It would have an effect on how white people think?'
Boy: 'Yes because when you're in class that's when you start to get all this prejudice stuff. You don't get a lot of black people's history, and what black people done.' (black children)
Boy: ' . . . We wanted to put the black people's point of view, the black people's side of history.' (black boy) 'You don't see things like this ever on television, because on Sunday its always things like Oliver Twist and all that.'
Teacher: 'Who controls TV?'
Boy: 'White men and few black people there.'
Boy: 'I saw on tele there is a programme what shows you who done what . . . whether its a man or woman, and mostly its just men. That's why I like Harriet Tubman because she done what a man and a woman done at the same time . . .
She's saying we're still *people*.'
(black children)

In the following section I shall refer to work done in seven schools, all of which follows a particular methodology. The initial method is similar to that outlined by Jim Pines in a BFI education pack 'Looking at images' (Pines, undated), by Marina Foster in 'Do children have views about stereotyping?' (Foster, 1979) and in my own article 'Stereotyping in the Primary Classroom', (Burgess, 1981). From these I have elaborated a model (shown on the opposite page) which attempts to summarise the processes which have been involved in extending anti-racist and anti-sexist consciousness in those schools.

Sharpening Awareness

In a first year junior classroom a mixed sex group of children took part in a science investigation. It was noticeable to the observer that (i) boys did most of the initiating and discussing; (ii) when girls attempted to take a lead they were prevented from doing so by boys; and (iii) the girls were resentful at being excluded but somewhat resigned to the situation which they saw as quite usual.

Observer: 'What was going on between you and the boys just then?'
Girl 1: 'Well the boys are doing the most.'
Girl 2: 'They were just letting us do the bad bits.'

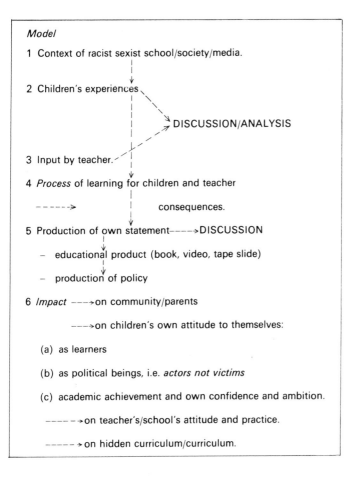

Model

1 Context of racist sexist school/society/media.

2 Children's experiences

DISCUSSION/ANALYSIS

3 Input by teacher.

4 *Process* of learning for children and teacher

- - - - -→   consequences.

5 Production of own statement - - - -→DISCUSSION

— educational product (book, video, tape slide)

— production of policy

6 *Impact* - - -→on community/parents

- - -→on children's own attitude to themselves:

(a) as learners

(b) as political beings, i.e. *actors not victims*

(c) academic achievement and own confidence and ambition.

- - - - -→on teacher's/school's attitude and practice.

- - - - -→on hidden curriculum/curriculum.

Girl *1*: 'We got really angry.'
Girl *2*: 'So we sat and crossed our arms . . . and didn't do anything.'
Girl *1*: 'We were unhappy.'
Girl *2*: 'They weren't letting us do anything.'

And the messages about sex role these seven year olds have got must give any teacher cause for concern.

Girl: 'I think boys are better than girls.'
Observer: 'Better at what?'
Girl *1*: 'Better at maths and all that stuff and counting.'
Observer: 'Do you?'
Girl *2*: 'Yes.'

Compare also the racist message which these black children had assimilated.

> *Teacher*: 'When you were younger – say in the infants and the teachers said you could draw a picture – and you did a drawing or painting of a person, what colour would you colour them in?'
> *Girl*: 'I colour them white.'
> *Teacher*: Why didn't you colour them brown?'
> *Boy*: 'Brown never looked good on them.'
> *Girl 2*: 'I wouldn't have coloured them brown because I don't see many pictures of brown people . . . and if I thought of a person immediately I would have thought of a white person, not a brown person.'

The impact of sexist and racist stereotypes on both the children's interaction and their participation in the learning situation is clear.

Bikes

Such discussion, in which children's own experience is linked to a study of materials, is an enjoyable exercise and can help to sharpen awareness about shared experiences of being stereotyped, and of how stereotypes are used to justify the exercising of power by one group over another.

I want to describe one such process in detail. It concerns a project on 'bikes' in which an anti-sexist element was introduced by looking at girls' and boys' use of bikes and at the images of bikes and bike riding in books.

First of all the children (seven, eight, nine and ten year olds) were asked to make a chart for their own class on bike ownership and bike usage. What emerged from this study was that whereas almost all the girls had bikes, fewer of them used them as much as the boys. What also emerged in discussion was that expectations about girls' and boys' behaviour were making a marked impact. Basically girls confined their use of bikes to cycling round the flats near their homes, going on errands. Whereas boys tended to gang up and travel further afield to 'the woods', and to do wheelies, skids and ramp riding, and also, as both girls and boys stated, to terrorise girls by 'skinning' them (riding too close to make them lose balance), putting things in their spokes, teasing them and harassing them with junior versions of sexual taunting.

> *Girl*: 'It is true that boys keep bothering girls on bikes because when I was little boys kept bothering me when I was with my sister.'
> *Teacher*: 'Were they doing it because you were a girl?'
> *Girl*: 'They were doing it just because I was riding my bike and they keep pushing me off. It was the boys who were doing it. They didn't push boys off.'
> *Boy*: 'A lot of boys don't like girls. And they wear skirts and that's why I think they're sissy, because boys always like to look up them and I think that's why they really hate girls, because they won't let them.'

The discussions prompted by these facts became quite heated, with some boys becoming very defensive but others shifting towards admitting the situation was 'not fair'.

The girls already knew it wasn't fair but were quite shy about confronting this *in mixed group* discussions.

Also some girls (especially in the older age group) had accepted that their role was not to compete in this sphere of sporting activity, which they related *directly* to their future roles as wife and mother.

> *Girl*: 'I reckon that really if you get married right, you got to learn to look after them – not how to fix bikes.'
> *Girl*: 'I want to be a nursery nurse.'
> *Observer*: 'So fixing bikes and things isn't important for girls?'
> *Girl*: 'I reckon that.'
> *Girl*: 'Men reckon that all that ladies should do is all the housework.'
> *Observer*: And is that what you want to do?'
> *Girl*: 'No.'

The project moved a stage further when the children had actually to dismantle a bike and learn how to 'fix' it (tyres, brakes, oiling, etc.).

Again there were marked differences in girls' and boys' enthusiasm for doing this and their familiarity with the tools and activities required. They made another chart which recorded who 'fixed' their bikes – males or females. With two exceptions all the amateur bike mechanics were men – brothers, fathers, uncles, grandads. And again the children related this to gender role.

> *Girl*: 'My mum's bike broke and it's up my auntie's house because her husband fixes things like that.'

Observer: 'She can't fix it herself?'
Girl: 'What! my mum?! She can't fix nothing.'
Observer: 'Why not?'
Girl: She don't know about nothing like that.'
Observer: 'Why is it that lots of women don't know that?'
Girl: 'Because they're not interested – only in things like cleaning.'
Girl: 'Maybe they reckon men should do that or boys.'
Girl: 'They've got too much work to do.'

To help the children in their questioning of why and how such differences come about, they were asked to look at all the books in their school library which had bikes in them and to make a block graph which tabulated whether males or females were shown riding, holding or 'fixing' the bikes. The results were dramatic with images of males and bikes outnumbering females in a ratio of ten to one.

This contrasted sharply with their previous graph which tabulated bike ownership and usage in their own class, where there were differences in usage but *not* the virtual absence of girls from the scene, as was the case in the books. The older age group looked specifically at books from the *infant* school and found the same stereotyped picture.

The question was then posed as to whether these books might help to *influence* children at an early age, which then meant girls did not have equal opportunity to ride bikes in the way they wished. So the next stage was to respond to this challenge and make books which had four different objectives. *The Fair Book of Bikes* made by a mixed group using photos of themselves riding and testing and servicing bikes, shows girls and boys doing the same activities – its purpose stated by the children.

'We made this book because in books they do not show the true number of girls that ride bikes. We wanted to stop this. We decided to make a book that was fair on boys and girls.'

The *All Girls Book of Bikes* done at the end of the project by an all-girl group, records, again using photographs, the girls' feelings and experiences about the subject of biking and their awareness of sexism.

'I like to ride my bike, why I don't know. I just do. But when I ride my bike I always see boys riding their bikes. I have never seen a girl there. The trouble is that boys think that they should have the racing-bikes and the flash bikes but it is not fair.'

'Girls have difficulties when boys come and say, "You cannot ride as good as me." Sometimes they chop you up. I was chopped up and I fell off my bike. I cut my leg. I went into my mum and I was crying. My mum bathed it. I stopped crying. I think they do this because of books. They show more boys on bikes than girls. I think girls should say, "We can ride as good as you," and ride off.'

Another book was designed page by page by another all-girl group as an infant reader and shows girls doing things with bikes (including wheelies and falling off but *not* crying). Their purpose was to show younger children that 'girls can be as good on bikes as boys – given the chance'.

A fourth series of photographs records the girls learning from a woman bike mechanic who spent a day at the school showing girls how to do basic maintenance and repairs. The girls found this a most enjoyable experience and the exclusion of the boys for part of the time by the woman mechanic was for all the children a lesson in positive discrimination for which, perhaps reluctantly, they began to understand the need. This is what two teachers said:

'I found it very interesting when Heidi was here and she was picking children from a mixed group to come and help her, the first three she picked were all girls and one of the boys I heard saying, "It's not fair – they're all girls" – and I think that exposure for them to that kind of bias in the opposite way to the normal sexist situation is something we should actually present the children with, though it's quite difficult to do this as the class teacher.'

'The tremendous difference is in the confidence of the girls, this is amazing. It's made a tremendous difference, this work.'

The impact on both the *teachers* involved in the work was to make them more aware of the need to develop specifically anti-sexist practice and to raise the question of whether space should be given in the organisation of these teachers for girls-only groups to operate from time to time.

'But I think you have got to have some planned activity, you have to have an opening that is within the experience of the children, and also it's much easier for the teacher. And once you've worked through something like this with the children you realise what a change it makes.'

Games

A similar model was adopted by another teacher doing a project
on games. The children both talked about the kind of games they
actually play and looked at the games shown in reading scheme
books.

> 'Because I want this world to change I want girls to play the boys
> things and the boys to play the girls things, see. Because we fed up
> with dolls and prams and things like that.'

In the discussions, the mixed group was dominated by boys'
contribution. They mainly defended the status quo with the girls
keeping silence, but an all-girls group quite quickly began to
express grievances about boys' domination of playground space,
the exclusion of girls (by the boys) from football games and the
indifference of most teachers and other staff to the problem.

> 'When we play football. The boys have a ball, right, and
> we say, "Can we play?" and the boys say, "No" and
> when we have a ball to play football, or netball or things
> like that they say, "Can we play?" and we say, "No" but
> they keep on joining in . . . and they kick us and next day
> you get a big bruise.'
>
> *Teacher*: 'What do you think the teachers and helpers ought to do
> about it?'
>
> 'They ought to do something about it. They should care
> about it. If he pushed us over they should take the one
> who pushed us over to the head, to Mrs B so that it's
> much fairer.'

Looking at Racism

So far I have used examples of children looking at sexism in
materials. An increasing number of teachers are doing this with
their children. Teachers often find it harder to approach looking
at racism in books, mainly because overall consciousness, as
white teachers, is not very developed. We don't notice the
racism. Yet teachers who have approached racism in materials
with children, have found black children to be quite aware, and
white children quickly to become so.

In the BBC *Scene* programme 'Why Prejudice?'[2] a group of
sixth formers discuss racism in the media among themselves and
with members of the black community and recall their own

experience of racism. Such work need not be restricted to sixth-form study. In one junior school a teacher decided to discover the level of consciousness of racist stereotyping and gave a group of children some books to look at, some of which had negative images of Asian or Afro-Caribbean peoples. The children were asked to write mini reviews of the books. They commented on the story-line presentation, interest, humour but not on racism. Then she showed them the video of 'Why Prejudice?'

After play, the children came back and were asked to reconsider the books. They proceeded to have over an hour of intense, serious discussion on racism and then some wrote critical appraisals of some books from this point of view. Some of these were then sent to publishers.

These children had been influenced, clearly, by what they had seen and heard and were able to apply it. In other words, they were *learning* to be aware.

That infants, too, can tackle similar work is shown in the All London Teachers Against Racism and Fascism (ALTARF) video *Racism, the 4th R* where a Hackney infant teacher is shown looking with the class at images in a book called *The Swimming Baths*.[3] The children had themselves commented on the book and were then encouraged to write to the publisher, thus making their criticism more than a classroom exercise.

They also went to their own local baths and took photographs. Their own book about swimming is altogether better than the original published book. As well as being a good exercise in early literacy, it is also an exercise in the early development of a critical consciousness.

'Unfairness' in Books

Some six year olds in a different class took a book called *Dressing Up*[4] from the 'Breakthrough to Literacy' scheme. They analysed this book first by counting the numbers.

'Me and Eleanor was looking at the *Dressing Up* book and we found out that there was twelve brown and thirty-nine white and it is not fair.'

They made some more sophisticated observations. They noticed that white children were featured most *prominently* in the activities described and were actually shown *doing* the dressing up.

'In all the pictures it is always the white person is always dressing up.'
'There can be brown firemen as well.'

They also noticed that on several occasions black children were portrayed in a servicing role.

'The black person is being kind of the servant in both the pictures. It wouldn't be fair if they just changed places, helping each other would be fair or do it yourself.'

These observations about books also contain statements about the injustice of a situation in which one group benefits at the expense of another. Primary age children have a strong moral sense and a sense of outrage at blatantly 'unfair' situations.

Neglected History

History topics in junior schools offer opportunities for developing a fuller understanding of present racist and sexist practices. It was with this particularly in mind that topics were chosen in the schools studied.

One concerned the life of Harriet Tubman, the second the life of Mary Seacole (both black women who made an important and neglected contribution to the history of their time and their people) and the third the life of Kathleen Wrasama, a black woman alive and living in London's East End. In all three cases the teachers deliberately chose the subject and introduced the material *which they had to obtain outside the school* from the black community.

The work of Harriet Tubman was part of a series of topics on famous people. The group working on Harriet Tubman were self-selected and all black.

By contrast the topic of Mary Seacole was part of a *whole school* topic on 'names' and the whole class (mainly white) were asked to do some research on Mary Seacole and to suggest possible answers to the question, 'Why was Florence Nightingale's name remembered and Mary Seacole's name forgotten?'

The work on Kathleen Wrasama's life was done by a whole class. Obviously the introduction of these black women into the history curriculum posed certain questions which children and teachers had to consider.

(i)   What evidence was there in the school libraries of the contribution of black people to history and the contribution of these women in particular?

(ii) Given that libraries had little or no information, why was this and what would we expect teachers to do? Pupils to do?

(iii) Was it a worthwhile exercise to study the lives of these women? If so, why? What in particular did children learn from this study?

(iv) Apart from learning some interesting historical facts, did the studies have wider implications for the children and what were they?

(v)   What was the impact of the work on others and how was this achieved?
      Teacher?
      School (other children, other staff)?
      Parents?
      Community?

These questions were approached in interviews with the children, their teachers and their parents. The interviews were tape-recorded and transcribed. They form the basis for this section.

The first thing to note is that the children were interested in the women's stories *as stories* and *also* for a variety of reasons which relate to their own consciousness of racism and sexism.

'I watched a programme called *Roots* and I wanted to find out more about black people and since she was a famous woman I did it on her.' (black girl)

'It's more enjoyable than Maths and English, because in that we learn the same things every day, at least I do, and you want to learn more things about the world and all that.' (white boy)

'I told my dad and he read it and you know how men always say women are the weaker sex and that . . . well my dad was amazed and he just said it was very good for my age what I did, . . . and what she did.'
'And he said she might well have saved one of our relations . . . or any black people relations.' (black boy)

Secondly, they approached discussions and investigations collaboratively but retained their individual emphasis and this was reflected in the end products and their final statements.

Third, the black children were not on the whole surprised by the absence of blacks from library encyclopaedias whereas some white children working on Mary Seacole were pretty horrified by the mountain of books on Florence Nightingale and the fact that *none* ever mention Mary. Black children showed themselves to be quite aware of racism, as this black parent states.

> *Mother*: 'She tried to find books on her in our local library, but she couldn't find anything.'
> *Interviewer*: 'What did she think about that – because one of the questions they were asked to think about was, "Why is this woman forgotten?"'
> *Mother*: 'She know that straight away. She say she feel it was because the lady was black and I tend to agree myself. But I ask her what she thinks first, because I don't like to put things in their mouth, I like them to think for themselves.'

In the following extract, the white children are partly grappling with this idea and also seeking other explanations.

> *Interviewer*: That's an interesting point, then, that you've raised because one of the ways we find out about the past is when its written down.
> *Girl*: 'You had to have a lot of money to get a good education.
> . . . in those days the soldiers wouldn't have that education because they were not given it so they couldn't have written about her even if they wanted to.'
> *Girl*: 'Only rich people wrote things down.'
> *Boy*: 'I think Mary was forgotten because the soldiers just wanted to get well again and lead their lives again and just get better and forget about it.'
> *Girl*: 'I think Mary Seacole was forgotten because her skin was black and they didn't like black people then.'
> *Interviewer*: 'Why didn't they like them then?'
> *Girl*: 'Because they used them as slaves.'
> Discussion with six children (four white and two black)

As well as delving into the nature of historical evidence and learning through one person's life, the children gained some insight into the period and the long history of racism. Two striking examples were of Mary being refused permission to go to the Crimea simply because she was black, and Harriet after the Civil War and freed from slavery, still being asked to travel in the luggage compartment on the train as seats in the 'free' North were reserved for whites.

The children were not slow to make connection with their present-day situations.

> Girl: 'I think because she was black the government wouldn't pay for her to go to the Crimea War but they would pay for Florence Nightingale to go.'
>
> Interviewer: 'Yes, discrimination. Do governments still practise that?'
>
> Boy: 'Yes, in South Africa they do. They still do it here, too.'
>
> Girl: 'We've got two rules in this school that the world hasn't got outside - no fighting and no name calling. They should have those rules outside.' (mixed group)

> 'I think we should learn about things like this because we must learn about our past and what has happened to us black people, and if white kids learn they might see how black people really are and not be prejudiced.' (black ten-year-old boy)

> 'I think Harriet was a brave woman and I think we need a Harriet Tubman for Margaret Thatcher.' (black nine-year-old girl)

The study had other implications for the children who took it most seriously, as is best evidenced by the fact that they quite voluntarily took the work out of school and involved parents and others in it.

> 'He seemed very surprised that a woman could . . . because just recently in our family we've been having tremendous rows about women's rights and girls' education . . . I went to the ILEA Conference on girls' education - as parent governor - B's heard a lot of these discussions and it was definitely the woman thing.

> 'I think he was tickled pink that this was a woman - and a black woman!' (from interview with white mother)

And the following is from an interview with a black mother:

> Interviewer: 'Do you remember doing any history at school?'
>
> Mother: 'Florence Nightingale, Christopher Columbus . . . people like that.
> 'We didn't learn a lot of things, things like these were kept back from us!
> 'That's why black people nowadays say a lot of things keep away from them when they were growing up. That's what a lot of people say now.

'Most black people here don't know anything about all
this because no one told them – so they can't demand
something you don't know about. I'll spread the news
around. History is important. More should be known
about it.

'You know, I keep asking when she come home,
"Have you seen that lady again – who is helping write
the book on Mary Seacole?" because I'm learning as
well.

'Yes, it's very important. I should have known
because I'm even from Jamaica. And if someone from
your country we should know more – but no – what
they taught us in school was all to do with England, or
slavery and the war. Nothing really about individual
people.'

Several children went to local libraries and one white father took
his daughter to the British Museum to try to find Mary Seacole's
autobiography.

An investigation using oral history was carried out in work
done on Kathleen Wrasama, a black woman who was interviewed for a BBC series called *Surviving*.[5] A video of this
programme was shown to two classes of junior children who
became very interested in her life story and decided to write
accounts of it and individually wrote to ask Kathleen herself to
visit the school so that they could question her. She replied to
each letter and did visit, and the children were able to find out
details of her early life and experience of racism that had not
been covered in the programme. The children made books and
painted pictures and were extremely impressed by the dignity
and lifelong struggle of this woman who had been brought to this
country as an orphan from Ethiopia at the beginning of the
century and treated with barbaric inhumanity by Christian
orphanages and foster parents alike because she was a black and
heathen savage.

This is part of an account by a black girl;

Her life was a misery. She even thought that God punished her
because of her colour. And Kathleen thought she was a freak, not a
proper human being. The girl went and tried to scrape her colour off
with turps. Kathleen ran away from the church missionary because
her life was fading away, she had to run away to get away from those
wicked people who is supposed to be the people of God . . . I think
that when Kathleen's real parents died the church missionary should
have thought of a black country before they took Kathleen to
Yorkshire.

A Poem for Kathleen
Kathleen, Kathleen, your heart suffers truth
The ventures you've been through
Always so alone
You on your own, no one else like you
You thought you was a freak
But I know its not true
The people in mind don't think about you
They want to find different friends,
different from you,
But Kathleen you have friends now,
Who cares for you.
(ten-year-old back girl)

Not only was the living account of an ordinary member of the black community a telling description of white British attitudes in colonial days, and therefore a part of the history of racism which children need to know, but Kathleen's spirit, lack of bitterness and hope for the future were an inspiring example to everyone.

In a letter to one of the children she wrote:

> It was so nice to read we should love one another black or white, and that you children are carrying the torch of understanding, hold it high, Sarah, don't let it blow out as you grow older. It shines bright in your school as my letters received from you shows.

There must be so much more that could be done by schools, work based on writing down the lives and thoughts of senior citizens – ordinary people, black and white, and thus writing the kind of history books that are so rarely produced by mainstream publishers.

Making a Response

The methodology of all these teachers was to enable the children to *make a response* to what they had observed and discussed, and in all cases writing their own history books was a vital part of the work.

The Harriet Tubman 'books' were written individually (with a great deal of consultation). They are a long, detailed and accurate account of her life written and illustrated by the children and printed for distribution to other classes. The children also made a tape-slide presentation for a school assembly (parents were present at this) and the tape-slide was also used by another teacher in the school. Copies of books and transcript of the tape-slide (the text was put together collabora-tively by the children from their own accounts) were sent to Alex Pascall of Radio London and the children were invited on to *Black Londoner's* programme to talk about it. In all cases, parents were impressed with the work and encouraging to the teacher.

The Mary Seacole work followed a similar format. It was specifically a response to the children's discovery that there was simply no information on this woman in the library. They wished to redress this by writing their own book. Again, the work was presented to the whole school (via an assembly theme) and went outside the school to have an impact on individual parents. A summary was also printed in a magazine for black youth called *Zinga*.

Part of the rationale for producing books is summarised in interview with one of the teachers who said:

'I think the methodology of this kind of work is the biggest problem in a way for teachers. Because if you are working in the classroom, you do want the children to be able to do some actual work and you do want to involve as many of the children as possible. So a discussion does not always fulfil those two things. Some children never take part; you get enormous difference in understanding concepts when presented just verbally.'

A Model for Anti-Racist and Anti-sexist Work

All the work described here has been done over the past few years, as teachers, becoming aware of their collusion in transmit-ting racist and sexist ideas to children, try to do something to counteract this which *involves* children and community.

The consciousness which even these young children are displaying has also been forged outside school and it is a reflection of struggles taking place in the community, and the growing awareness of children of the disadvantage and conflicts they meet in society.

As primary school teachers, we are familiar with the idea of starting with children's experiences and building on them. However, all too often in multicultural education we start not with actual experience but with a stereotypical assumption about that experience. We may assume that black children like music and dancing, assume that Asian children are religious and conformist, assume that girls will be interested in subjects requiring sensitivity rather than technical skills.

We also tend to define for children what kinds of experiences we as teachers are interested in, and this means that communication tends to be one way. Children will not ram down our throats things they have come to expect we don't want to hear.

Our reluctance to give the children and parents a voice is the reason why so many teachers still persist in the notion that racism does not exist in school and that white children 'don't notice' racial differences, or black children 'don't care' about racial abuse.

With regards to sexism, perhaps we are becoming more aware of the extent of the problem, simply because there are many women involved in education and able to say something, whereas racism has effectively kept the power structures of schools white, with black teachers and parents having little voice. If we are genuinely to look at children's experiences, then we will have to look at their experiences specifically as girls, boys, as black or white, as working class or middle class. We will have to include their experience of the media and the impact on even young children of our racist and sexist culture. We will have to look at their experience of discrimination, not just 'celebrate' cultural diversity; look at the experience of being an oppressed group, not just the 'identity' of being black or a girl. We are talking about processes, but the work described has also involved products. These are important, since they indicate to the children, to the teacher, and, very importantly, to parents and to colleagues, even superiors, that something worthwhile has been achieved.

The product serves different aims for the different participants in education. First, it is tangible communication of children's individual or collective statement about the intellectual work they have been engaged in. It is *their* evidence. Second, it is a recognition by the teacher that their work/ thoughts are worthy of being properly recorded. It is *her* evaluation of their evidence. Third, it is a proof that anti-racist or anti-sexist work is not just 'hot air' or an extra luxury. It relates to the curriculum and the basic concerns of teachers and children. It is part and parcel of the *learning situation* as well as the social situation of children. Fourth, it is important that parents see something concrete, as we cannot expect them to take on trust that the work which has been done is not a diversion from 'real' work. Fifth, it is important if the work is to have an impact beyond the classroom walls – into the school as a whole and into the community – that the work done is presented in as many and varied ways as teachers and children can imagine. Children must see themselves as capable of communicating – as active learners and political beings – and of being as capable of this as the slickest Fleet Street reporter whom they will learn to criticise.

The starting point, then, for an anti-racist or anti-sexist approach is still the children's experience, but viewed widely in the context of the society and school. In addition to children's experience, there must also be an input by the teacher. The nature of this input is determined by the teacher's position in the school, the demands of the curriculum, and by the teacher's own ideas and awareness. This latter element of choice is important, because the process of learning is a joint one. The teacher's consciousness and practice must change, too.

Because racism and sexism are so embedded in our British culture it is often difficult for teachers to recognise their impact and even more difficult to work out how, as teachers, we should counteract them. We ourselves are part of the problem. Our awareness of this is the first crucial step towards looking for changes. There are those of us who are trying to put aside our professional defences and listen to other voices in education – to listen to children, to listen to voices from the black community, from the women's movement; and there are growing pressures on schools that will force us to listen – and, dare I say it, take sides.

In this chapter I have tried to describe what some primary school teachers have done in their classrooms to develop in themselves and their pupils both a clearer consciousness of the issues, and an ability to act towards changes, however small they may be. I would wish to thank all those teachers, children and parents whose work or words I have quoted.

> There is no such thing as a neutral education process. Education either functions as an instrument to facilitate the integration of the young generation into the logic of the present system and bring about conformity to it, or it becomes 'the practice of freedom' the means by which men and women deal critically and creatively with reality and discover how to participate in the transformation of their world. (Richard Schaul in the foreword to Paulo Friere's *Pedagogy of the Opressed*).

NOTES

1 For further information on Harriet Tubman the following books may prove useful:
   HEIDESH, M. *A woman called Moses.* New York: Bantam.
   MCGOVERN, A. *'Wanted – Dead or Alive': A true story of Harriet Tubman.* New York: Scholastic Books.
   STERLING, D. *Black Foremothers – Three Lives.* New York: The Feminist Press.

2 'Why Prejudice?' *Scene* Series, BBC Schools Television.

3 *Racism: the 4th R.* Video made by All London Teachers against Racism and Fascism and available from ALTARF, c/o Lambeth Teachers' Centre, Santley Street, London, SW4.

4 The *Breakthrough to Literacy* reading scheme is published by Longmans. *Dressing Up* was published in 1971 and reprinted in 1974.

5 In an interview for the BBC series *Surviving*, Kathleen Wrasama told of her life in the East End of London. She described the way things had changed and what had remained the same in her long life and commented on the position of black people in contemporary society.

9 Multicultural and Anti-racist Approaches to the Teaching of Science in Schools

Terry Mears

There are many possible interpretations of the term 'multicultural' and of what may be called 'school science', just as there are many views on what schooling is for and for what range of pupils serious education is appropriate. The first task, therefore, will be to examine some of these interpretations before suggesting possible ways of bringing some new ideas to the classroom. It is assumed here that a multicultural approach does not weaken an anti-racist commitment, but it is realised that there are strong arguments that multiculturalism can serve just that function.

Most children who learn any science at school do not become scientists, so a consideration of what a multicultural or anti-racist science curriculum might look like is not primarily, therefore, about job opportunity but about general education. In addition, it can be stated that we are not talking about special educational provision for black or other ethnic minority pupils. It cannot be stressed too firmly that the position adopted here is that the problem does not lie with black children but rather with a science curriculum that still enshrines ideas of white superiority. The task is to re-shape the curriculum for all pupils so that it becomes a means of dismantling racism, sexism and class prejudice, and better meets knowledge of what science is and where it fits into the world outside the classroom.

Scientific statements are sometimes claimed to be factual, objective and invariant over space and time, i.e. water has a boiling point of 100°C everywhere and for all time. For a start, the boiling point of water is not invariant, and even if it were, this begs all the other questions. Modern science could not have developed its present scope and power with such a naïve idea of its own method and such weak philosophical underpinning. Modern science depends on flexible thinking. In the twentieth century, scientists have been forced to abandon simple ideas of matter, objectivity, energy and much of the mid-nineteenth-century world view where our school science has its origins. Science is not, by nature, value free, context independent and universal. Nor can school science, despite pressures to keep sociological, cultural, economic and political perspectives out of the science classroom, be deprived of its social and historical context.

School Science

As is common knowledge, no practising scientist can keep abreast of developments outside a narrow range of specialisation, such is the speed of change in the scientific community. Thus it is hardly surprising that school science does not make a simple match with real science. This does not prevent pressure on the curriculum of schools to feed the requirement for narrow specialists and to accept an order of superiority among science subjects which operates hierarchically in terms of carefully maintained boundaries with maths, physics, chemistry, biology, zoology, botany, integrated science and general science comprising school science and having roughly that order in terms of status. (Many aspects of science in the world outside school such as geology, meteorology, astronomy, metallurgy, food science, ecology, have as yet no clearly established space in the school curriculum.)

Even where science departments are engaged in integration, prestige usually still attaches to the separate disciplines and anyway advanced studies require a reversion to the individual subject areas. What we see here are the consequences of the traditional separation of: theoretical and practical science; science and technology; 'hard' and 'soft' science; science and humanities.

It is interesting to note that there appear to be correlations between the 'hardness' or 'softness' of a science subject as traditionally understood and the interest and competence shown by males and females at school – the more abstract the more male defined, seems to be the rule.

Historically, many of the arguments used to keep blacks and women from power and education have overlapped. Scientific language and imagery seem to enshrine a mentality which can be seen as oppressive from a range of perspectives: black, female or working class. Although the race, gender and class biases are to a certain extent inseparable, in this chapter I am primarily concerned with finding ways of overcoming an assumed white superiority enshrined in the science curriculum.

A Multicultural Approach

It is the contention of this chapter that a multicultural commitment in the strongest sense has very far-reaching implications for school science and that a multicultural commitment introduces a social, historical and political context for science teaching which is still usually evaded.

There can, of course, be a multiplicity of approaches with a wide range of political flavours. There is no one radical, or liberal stance, or even a conservative one. The map of world science is being redrawn. Science education can and must rise to the challenge but it will mean having to look at philosophies of science and revisit concepts like objectivity, value freeness, scientific method or methods, positivism, behaviourism, dialectical interactions, relativity and biological determinism and many others if we are adequately to rise to the challenge posed by a multicultural approach.

Similarly, the term 'Western science' as a synonym for modern science is an arrogant and unjustified claim to precedence on the part of those with the power to make the rules. However, given the education that our science teachers have received and the demands of existing curricula and timetables, the ignorance of anthropological and historical evidence to the contrary is not surprising.

Anthropological Approaches

The work of Needham (1979, 1980) and many other scholars is revealing a rich set of interconnections between east and west (and north and south). The contributions of Chinese, Indian, African, Arabic cultures to modern science are no longer in doubt. All the time new evidence comes to light of unsuspected sophistication among people deemed to be outside the range of modern civilisation (assumed to be Western). Anthropological work, for example that of Lévi-Strauss in *The Savage Mind* (Lévi-Strauss, 1968), reveals that cultures with belief systems foreign to our own need to be approached with a far greater humility than has commonly been the case. One of the more accessible areas for this sort of enquiry is medicine. Already acupuncture and many other traditional medical systems and herbal lores reveal that Western medicine is not the only branch of knowledge of biological matters worthy of respect. Illich in *Limits to Medicine: Medical Nemesis* gives a wealth of material on the limits and contradictions of Western approaches to medicine (Illich, 1976).

History and Philosophy of Science

Work on the history of Western science reveals a rich web of connections between ideas about the nature of reality and political and religious assumptions. The work of Capra (1975, 1983) and Bohm (1980), among other physicists, suggest extraordinary relationships between Taoist, Buddhist, Hindu and other non-Western religious/philosophical traditions and 'new' ideas about the nature of reality revealed by modern physics.

The ideas of Popper (1969), Lakatos (1970), Kuhn (1962) and Feyerabend (1974, 1982), among other philosophers of science, reveal a vision of actual scientific method and history vastly different from that usually given to pupils.[1]

School and Society

We may wish to ask for what reason children are learning science in school. Some teachers think of it as primarily about method, experiment and reasoning – as a discipline in some ways akin to Greek and Latin in the classical curriculum. Other teachers see an essentially practical function, to do with understanding the world we live in, how things work in the home and outside.

Given that we have a commitment to equal opportunity, are we not obliged to try and match the areas studied at school with those predominant outside school? What in schools at present matches the predominance of biochemistry, biotechnology, energy science, genetic engineering, microelectronics, robotics, metallurgy, plastics research? Similarly, what about logic, systems analysis, cybernetics, anthropology, psychology, eth-

ology/sociobiology? What about history (and geography) and
philosophy of science? Are children being given the conceptual
equipment necessary to be involved in what is happening in the
world? The point being made here is not that schools should be
producing education to fit the needs of industries, (indeed,
current values might need to be questioned) but that this is part
of the reality of science as modern industry.

Some Practical Suggestions: Changes in Perspective

How did we arrive at our present idea of the sun rising in the
'east'? Would it seem different from the Pacific? After all, east
and west are directions rather than areas of the world. The
scientific basis for mapping is a fertile source of lesson material
and maps are a revealing source of ethnocentric bias. Why
should a map not be upside down, for example? Much useful
work can be done by comparing the concepts on which the
Mercator and other traditionally used projections are based
with those on which the newer Peters' projection and the
Buckminster Fuller Dymaxion map are constructed.

As well as looking at the science which underlies geographical
practices, it is possible to find useful material in science-fiction
writing which suggests alternative mental maps of the world
which can be used in the classroom. Keith Roberts (1984)
proposes a possible world where the Reformation never happened and technology is thus completely altered. There are
many other novels and short stories[2] which take a perspective of
science which is integrated into belief systems different from
our dominant ones. They can be used to stimulate imagination
and a critical perspective on how science is used now. Concepts
of progress and modernisation can be investigated in a more
rounded way.

Making Connections

It will already be clear that enabling pupils to make connections
in areas of thinking which have international and multicultural
significance has implications for greater co-operation between
departments. Many of the discussion areas in social studies,
human biology, geography, citizenship, cannot adequately be
tackled if the scientific perspectives remain for the pupil

ethnocentric and narrowly defined within the concerns of the science department. Mathematics has a key role to play here not only because statistics are used, and abused, in areas of race sensitivity but also in terms of fuller cultural and historical understanding. Lancelot Hogben's approach in *Mathematics for the Million* and *Science for the Citizen* shows a strong sense of the interconnections between different cultures' activity and their mathematics and science, which is all too often missing in more modern textbooks (Hogben 1938, 1967).

Experimental work based on the sensitive adaptation to local conditions of 'Third World Science' materials suggests that it is possible to help children to see that science is a world-wide activity which has to be adapted to circumstance and is not only dependent on high-level technologies. Encouraging results are reported (Watts, 1983; Williams, 1984) in the use of materials on topics which involve relatively simple things and ordinary people. Topics explored so far are: Carrying loads, Cement, Charcoal, Clay pots, Dental care, Distillation, Energy converters, Fermentation, Food preservation, Fuels, Housing, Iron smelting, Methane digestors, Natural dyes, Natural fibres, Salt, Soap, Useful plants, Vegetable oils. There is, of course, some risk involved that the materials may suggest that the technologies of some countries are quaint by comparison with larger-scale technologies. They provide, however, valuable ways of examining 'intermediate', 'alternative' or small-scale technologies and their place within different cultures.

It may be helpful here to give a warning that at all costs science teachers have to avoid constructing an association between 'big science', high technology in 'advanced' countries, and second-rate science and inferior technologies in 'underdeveloped' countries (although some approaches are manifestly more capital intensive than others). Science teachers have as much to learn as, say, geographers and historians, about ways of perceiving 'north and south', the 'third world' and issues of 'development' and exploitation. The journal, *Contemporary Issues in Geography and Education*, gives some indication of the sort of bias in textbooks and in their own unexamined ideas and use of language that science teachers might guard against.[3]

Viewing Science Critically

It can be seen as of central importance for the science teacher to encourage a healthy suspicion of the sorts of images of science newspapers and magazines and there is every reason why this should extend to a critical viewing of film and other material that comes into schools. For a start, the story that is told about science is not always scientifically accurate. Secondly, somewhere along the line, consideration of exploitation, and of the situation of rich and poor within and between nations must occur. Science teachers have a responsibility to give pupils tools by which they can recognise, and counter, vested interest and propaganda. Neutrality is not a viable position. To argue that you have no political stance is to favour the status quo. Very few practising scientists can remain unaware of the dependence of much current research on multi-national and military budgets, nor of the bounds that such restrictions impose. It is not reasonable for school children to remain in ignorance of such factors.

Resources

The development of this critical awareness is dependent on the availability of information. Compared with the amount of new material that is now appearing which reviews the curriculum from a multicultural standpoint in other subjects, science is at present poorly resourced. There is a wealth of material in the form of film, books, teaching packs, courses and so on in religious studies. It can be claimed that science is at least as sensitive an area. Practical help for science teachers could be in the form of book lists, digests, recent scientific theories and developments, extracts from relevant articles, particularly those relating to areas which media coverage has distorted but stimulated interest in. The dizzying speed of growth in scientific change will be discussed later, but suffice it to say that an impossible burden is placed on those teachers who have to pass on to the next generation what science is all about. An even more impossible burden is placed on the shoulders of those children who want to connect science curricula to what science is all about in the world.

What the Children Know

At the risk of stating the obvious, and acknowledging the constraints of curricula time and teachers' varying inclination for discussion-related teaching, teachers can take advantage of the fact that children have a lot to offer as well as to learn. In many ways they can be more attuned than their teachers to what modern science is all about. (Computer technology is a case in point.) Those about to leave school have a vested interest in relating their curricula to the world outside, with or without solid employment to follow.

We are frequently reminded by politicians that Britain's future lies with its young and that they require an education fitted to the requirements of the times – the economic realities and the social realities. Germany, Japan, the United States (even the Soviet Union sometimes) are held up as models.

'Invention and technical expertise will put the UK back as a world leader.'
'We need more scientists and engineers.'
'Every child shall have access to a computer.'

We are continually exhorted to a new, white-hot technological revolution. But a great many school children are also aware of problems and contradictions in the world – many of them brought about by a certain sort of science: massive food production and surplus as against massive starvation; great developments in medicine and sickness of new kinds; robots, computer games, opportunities for sophisticated leisure along with perpetual unemployment, vandalism and urban poverty; great advance in building materials and technology and massive housing crisis; techniques for averting congenital malformations and genetic engineering horrors; junk food, health food, anorexia nervosa, food allergies, chemical pollution.

And, of course, there are the 'population explosion', 'destruction of the environment', nuclear power and 'the bomb' (to use journalistic jargon). There are massive problems here, which the presciption 'more scientists' doesn't meet. All the provocative areas mentioned above are related at one time or other to issues of east/west, black/white, oppressor/oppressed.

Primary School and Secondary School Science

Younger pupils have been at a certain advantage up to now because the innovations in primary education following on from the Plowden Report – the integrated day, learning through awareness of the local environment, lessening of competitiveness and so on, have enabled some science to be integrated into the curriculum as part of the local culture of the individual school. At the primary and middle-school level the more philosophical questions as to what science is, why we do it, how we do it, and what it is for, still hold sway (at least in theory). In primary education, we are talking about an activity which is for everyone. As writing, drawing, reading, making music are for everyone, so are solving problems, making experiments, drawing conclusions from evidence (again, at least in theory).

At the primary level there is the possibility that the constitution of the classroom affects what is taught in a major way. The child may bring contributions from family and background. All the surroundings of the school can affect the educational process. Also, as the junior teacher is covering a range of subject areas, the effect of campaigns against sexism and racism in children's books or against too much ethnocentricity in history, can hardly go unnoticed. For example, the revolutionary revelation that Columbus did not discover America can work as a fertile seed across the disciplines, spreading a necessary humility in the face of the world's real history.

Secondary science is, by contrast, defined by a much more abstract science curriculum. Any specialist secondary teacher tied to exams and marking and the passing on of a specialised vocabulary, is busy enough – add to that the special discipline problems arising out of potentially dangerous practical work and it's not hard to understand a reluctance on the part of science teachers to recast science teaching to meet the demands of a multicultural society.

Repair Work on a Divided Society

However confident we may be in the good sense of the children we teach and in the validity of the programme of reform that is needed, there remains the question of feasibility. Is it really feasible fundamentally to reorganise our curricula, introduce new materials, replace out-dated textbooks and apparatus and integrate subject areas, given present financial constraints and an apparent lack of commitment to justice and equality in the prevailing social order? The following remarks may strike some readers as being excessively cynical but practising teachers often get fed up with having to do repair work for a divided society.

It has been suggested that curricula stay as they are for a very good reason. It does not require excessive cynicism to see that general education has always satisfied power interests whether of church or state or both. The conditions which required a healthy, disciplined, literate and numerate workforce have changed and school obviously serves many interests which are not primarily educational. If the educational system were to prove capable of producing a large number of children, literate and numerate in modern sciences and fitted to tackle those tasks which require a scientific solution, many political and economic changes of great magnitude would be required before there was a place for them. Schools cannot possibly bear the burden of social, technological/scientific change on their own. So it has to be faced honestly that a shift in science curriculum away from the values currently enshrined is part of a struggle about control of resources, mental and physical. This informs both the crisis in Western science in terms of resource distribution and the crisis within science education.

It has been noted frequently that the development of science has led to increasing specialisation, increasing amounts of scientific literature, and a consequent increasing gap between layperson and scientist. This is clearly true for the conventionally educated speaker of English and much more so for the uneducated, the poor, sick, the underdeveloped, the oppressed, the peripheral and so on.

Many indices have shown an exponential curve shooting rapidly towards infinity around the end of the twentieth century, whether we measure by books or papers published on scientific matters, money spent on research and development, graduates needed, inventions patented or whatever. One such extrapolation – that the weight of scientific papers published will be more than the weight of planet Earth soon after 2000, is clearly not to be taken too seriously. It stands, however, as a provocative reminder of the amount of information piling up. Whether it's stored on paper, or tape, or chips misses the point. The point is that, to most of the world, it's a meaningless forecast. How much *useful* material is there which can help a food problem, an erosion problem, or a transport problem? How much of what is useful can filter through to those who have the problems to solve? Given limited material and educational resources, how much unnecessary duplication does there have to be? There are moral and ethical problems here which school science has to confront along with science outside the school.

One such area of duplication which has attendant ethical questions is dissection. How many rabbits need to be bred (or frogs, dogfish, etc.) for the endlessly repeatable first steps with a scalpel? Although some wish to be nurses, doctors or surgeons, veterinary or otherwise, many don't. There are areas of religious prohibition which have to be taken seriously, as does the whole question of experimenting on animals. Although this is not the place for a disquisition on alternative medicine or comparative religion, we should bear in mind that the dominant 'no nonsense' Christian/scientific world view of the eighteenth and nineteenth centuries, and (if we judge from our schooling) late twentieth century too, is neither universal nor 'correct'.

'Good' Science and 'Bad' Science

Where, then, should science teachers begin? Arguably, it must be with our own thinking and nowhere is this more difficult than in relation to racism which will here stand as an example of just what we have to take on more generally. For if we are serious about combating racism in all its forms, then, however awkward it is for us, we should consider carefully any evidence that any school subjects initiate or perpetuate ideas about the natural superiority or inferiority of any subgroups of humankind or their biological limits to achieving civilisation as currently defined. This is of particular embarrassment to school teachers, given the overwhelming commitment of schools to IQ testing and other forms of quantification and grading which can so easily justify and develop dormant prejudice. Science teachers are no more immune that anyone else to racial prejudice. Science teachers are often all too ignorant of what evidence exists now in areas of race, genetics, biological determinism. There is more to all this than the legacy of discredited Burt and of Jensen. A reading of *The Mismeasurement of Man* (Gould, 1984) could open many teacher's eyes to the racist history of English and American (in particular) biology, anthropology and psychology. Scientific racism was not a historical aberration occurring only in Hitler's Germany.

Luckily science as a historical set of disciplines can correct itself. Good science can drive out bad science. Many concerned with education against racism regard this subject as more critical than some others mentioned hitherto. Racist ideas are again given credence in many quarters including, obviously, schools. Sociobiology as a subject has caught media attention. Dangerous philosophical confusions abound between intelligence or aggression as descriptions of behaviour in social contexts, and intelligence or aggression as innate genetic components. Arguments *against* the popularisers of tendentious and often propagandist views on human nature tend to be underrepresented in the media or else caricatured as the politically motivated views of extremists who deny obvious human differences and wish for a society of totalitarian uniformity. Rose, Lewontin and Kamin (1984) cover this ground thoroughly in *Not in Our Genes*.

At one level, multicultural and anti-racist science already exists. In Athens in 1981, under the auspices of UNESCO, a group of scientists from France, India, Israel, Mexico, Japan, Tunisia, Russia, Senegal, working in fields as diverse as pure mathematics and anthropology, met to examine pseudo-scientific theories invoked to justify racism and racial discrimination. Their findings were published by Unesco under the title *Racism, Science and Pseudo-Science*. Their collective conclusion makes it clear that it is central to the interests of science and scientists that political and ethical issues are addressed:

> Those engaged in scientific activity bear a major responsibility for the social future of their contemporaries. Where racism is concerned, this responsibility involves political and ethical choices. Scientific research, particularly in the field of the human and social sciences, should always be based on respect for human dignity.
>
> Recognition of the risks to mankind implicit in certain applications of science should lead not to a rejection of science but rather to the fostering among the public at large of a genuinely scientific attitude, that is, an attitude based not on an accumulation of certainties but on the cultivation of a critical spirit and the continual challenging of accepted views. The struggle against racism in all its forms calls for the extensive involvement of scientists in the fostering of these attitudes, making use in particular of education systems and the media.
>
> There is a need therefore for scientists, whatever their differences or divergencies of viewpoint, to strive to maintain the objectivity that will ensure that their work and conclusions cannot be used as the basis for falsifications and interpretations detrimental to mankind (UNESCO, 1983).

It remains for those concerned with 'school science' to take on the challenge.

NOTES

1 Those who are not familiar with the arguments within the History and Philosophy of Science and the polemics between the above, are referred to a handy summary by RAVETZ, J., in *Radical Philosophy*, Summer 1984.
   Some of Feyerabend's provocative ideas in *Science in a Free Society* on the reality status of science and superstition, and Robin Horton's comparison of African religious beliefs and modern scientific concepts provoke revaluations. While it is not being proposed here that all beliefs and world views have the same status, it suggests that a less ethnocentric approach to science would find it harder to erect clear barriers around 'science' so as to keep out the 'primitive', the 'superstitious', the 'mythical'.

2 See, for example, among many science-fiction novels:
   MILLER, W. J. (1976) *Canticle for Leibowitz*. New York: Bantam.
   LEGUIN, U. (1974) *Dispossessed*. London: Panther Books.
   LEM, S. (1978) *Solaris*. Harmondsworth: Penguin Books.

3 *Contemporary Issues in Geography and Education* is the journal of the Association for Curriculum Development in Geography and is available from the Mailing Secretary, Geography Department, University of London Institute of Education, 20 Bedford Way, London, WC1H OAL.

10 The Role of the School Library in Multicultural Education

Gillian Klein

Many of the schools that have responded to the demands of education for a multicultural society are the same schools that have overturned their more hierarchical structures and re-defined their aims and their curriculum. They are often also the schools which, recognising that there is no single received body of knowledge which can simply be passed on to the new generation, base their pedagogical approach on resource-based learning.

This means that materials will be a focus of concern and so will the pupils' skills in making use of them. This chapter is concerned with schools of this nature – still only a tiny proportion – in which it is clear that an effective school library can make an active contribution to multicultural education, that is education for a multicultural society.

No librarian, however, can determine the school curriculum or classroom practice. If the school does not see as part of its educational responsibility the preparation of our future citizens for their place in the multicultural society and in a shrinking and increasingly inter-dependent world, no amount of relevant material in the library, subversively promoted, will have much effect.

On the other hand, the librarian, in her* role as information agent to the staff, can help raise awareness of the issues,

* I have used the pronoun 'she' for librarians, even though it is by no means true that all librarians are women. And, following Margaret Spencer's example of avoiding confusion, I have called all students 'he', even though not all are boys.

providing them with resources for their own information, such as this book. She can scan *The Times Educational Supplement,* other educational journals, and those dealing specifically with multicultural teaching and sex equality,[1] for pertinent articles, particularly those in specific subject areas, and put them into appropriate hands. She can alert staff to policy documents published by their local authority, or by others; she can heighten their sensitivity by stocking and encouraging them to read novels that will offer *them* insights into life in other cultures, or experiences of discrimination in the UK or US;[2] she can use her channels for acquisition of information to pass on documentation of initiatives in other schools that may be appropriate in hers. With a fixed base, a light timetable for classes and, one would hope, some taught administrative skills, the librarian is well placed to take the initiative in developing and supporting in-service programmes for education in a multicultural society. The librarian, whatever her training, should see herself, and be seen by her colleagues, as part of the professional team in the school. She should be automatically involved in staff activities, relevant committees and curriculum development work. She must have opportunities for frequent contact, both formal and informal, with all the teaching staff.

To find these conditions, these very separate criteria, all operating in the same school, is still a rarity. That is: a school open to self-evaluation, development and innovation and with a commitment to preparing all pupils for our multicultural society, a school which, at the same time, values the role of resources and resource-based learning and recognises the special professional contribution of the librarian. It would be misleading to suggest that school libraries all over the country are supporting the development of education in a multicultural society; they are not. There are even schools where faculties have taken the work of a multicultural curriculum and approach a considerable way forward – and left the library far behind. But what follows is an attempt to identify the conditions under which the library *can* play a dynamic role in the development of a multicultural curriculum in the school, based on observation of a number of schools where it *is* happening. And if issues of equality of sex and class are also taken on in school and library, the same conditions will create a favourable climate for their advancement also.

The Structure and Organisation of the Library

The 'central' position of the library should also be a physical reality. Not all materials need reside in the central collection, however: stock should move out to the children and teachers, through frequently changed classroom collections and through providing facilities for displaying library materials other than in the library.

Within the libraries, certain conditions appear axiomatic. It is the rule rather than the exception these days that the school library is an attractive and welcoming place. Plants have replaced plaster busts of Shakespeare; posters the portraits of heads from an authoritarian era. Books themselves are bright, colourful and often fairly ephemeral; Chivers' bindings are out of place on today's shelves, whatever their durability and dignity. Even so, it is still perfectly possible for a school library of the 1980s to signal that it is only there to serve a select few of the school population – the bookworms, who are generally middle-class creatures. Care and attention must be given to ensuring that the library appears welcoming and relevant to *all* the school population, whatever their race, religion, language or class. With some thought, a little sensitivity, it is easily done: those posters can be about events in the community, can be in the languages of the students; the periodicals can reflect the cultures, languages and concerns of the community; among the books on display can be those on subjects relevant to the students and, again, some in home languages. The same languages or at least some of them, can be used for the guiding to and labelling of the shelves – 'Spanish – Español', for example, or the Urdu word for 'Islam' beside the English. If required, parents or students may be involved in writing the labels; they may also wish to try their hands at the prominently displayed notice about 'How to find what you want in this library' – the one that dispels that forbidding library mystique and that ends, 'if you can't find what you need, ask the librarian'.

There are a large number of complex chores[3] that go into the day-to-day running of a school library. Materials must be ordered and then processed. Next, they have to be organised for loan, involving effective guidance to their location and the maintenance of an issue system, which should include an efficient reserve system as this is one way to make borrowers feel that the library really is concerned to serve them (and this is particularly easy to operate in a school). The shelves need occasional checking, tidying and weeding; stocktaking may be expected; reports may have to be written. The librarian needs the skills and knowledge to operate all these mechanical tasks so that she can do them in a minimum of time. It is all too easy for the 'housework' to take over, but all the chores are merely a means to an end and not an end in themselves. Clerical assistance should be available where necessary, so that the main thrust of the librarian's work can be in selecting materials appropriate to her users and to the aims of the school. This means keeping herself informed about the contents of her stock, so that she can implement a fundamental service of any library: to supply the right resource to the right reader at the right time.

Mention must here be made of the Dewey Decimal Classification in relation to the multicultural society. All classification schemes classify knowledge, not the materials themselves – as such, they can be no more than a guide. For their part, librarians are trained in classification skills, which means that they consider which will be the most appropriate place in the schedules for each item, in terms of both the topics covered within that item and also where the clientele are most likely to look for it.

There are evidences of both racism and sexism in the Dewey system of classification,[4] though 'abortion' has in recent editions been moved from its position under 'murder'. There is no doubt about even the most updated edition's monocentricism, however – Anglo-American to be precise. To illustrate: out of the ten main classes, the 200s is devoted to religion and of this, numbers 220 – 289 deal exclusively with Christianity. One tenth of the class is left to cover 'All Other Religions' (290–299), including Buddhism and Islam, Judaism, Janism and Hinduism. As for Shintoism, Taoism and Confucianism, they do not even rate numbers of their own, but are tagged on merely as 'other religions'.

Language (400s) and Literature (800s) follow a similar pattern. The same amount of space (490–499) is given to all the world's non-European languages, as is given to English alone (420–429). There is little the librarian can do to counter these imbalances, short of rewriting the classification scheme, which is a lifetime's task! But she should be constantly on the alert for manifestations of bias, particularly with regard to:

(i) *Terminology* Derogatory terms have been expunged from later editions of Dewey – but possibly not from the subject index to the library's classified catalogue. And certain outdated descriptive terms still occur, e.g. for 301.44, 'hobos, tramps, untouchables, hippies'.

(ii) *Position* The objective of the classification system is not only to bring together all material on the same subject but also to bring related topics close together. In terms of diverse cultures, Dewey fails on both counts. And where women's studies is concerned, no classification scheme could be expected to bring the range of social, political, health and educational issues under one umbrella category. All library classification schemes are classifications of *knowledge*, not of the books.

If each book were to appear in each place on the shelves to which its content relates, multiple copies would be needed of practically every one. The skill of the classifier rests in deciding where the book will be most useful for that particular collection and clientele, so determining its place on the shelves. But the facility for retrieving the book in the context of other locations in the scheme are provided to an infinite degree by the catalogue or information storage scheme. In response to cultural diversity, cross-referencing in this way is essential: Caribbean cookery books, then, shelved with other recipe books in the 600s, would be indexed also under country, in the 900s. Printed lists of the materials available on specific topics may be another solution, so long as these are updated or abandoned before they become inaccurate.

(iii) *Arrangement* There is no rule that all library materials need be arranged in strict classified – or alphabetical – order; in fact they seldom are. Selections by age, to support topic work, or to relate to an outside event such as a space-probe, are a common feature of vital libraries. Resources can be pulled out of all ten classes and set together, either as a temporary display or permanently, if that is how they will be required and used. But because of its expandability, flexibility, regular updating to incorporate new areas of knowledge and reassuring match with public libraries, it seems unavoidable to continue classifying any sizeable resource collection in schools by Dewey.

(iv) *Labelling* Intelligent and imaginative labelling can do much to conceal the monocentricism of the schedule headings. Labels should be related to the school curriculum and to the reading interests of the library users rather than to the main Dewey classes: a label, for example, for 'Hinduism', even though it is a tiny subsection, in a school which studies comparative religion.

All these details of organisation are merely to facilitate the functioning of the library so that it can fulfil its fundamental role: *to support learning in the school and, one hopes, enrich the leisure lives and extend and deepen the insights and understanding of the pupils.*

Supporting Learning

In supporting learning in the school, the librarian becomes an active teaching agent. She may begin with the student by matching his information needs to the appropriate resource, but this is only the first step. The next is to help the student to define his precise requirements, and then to locate for himself the relevant books and resources. He may need further help to make sense of the information in them. But the librarian's task is *still* not complete; nor will it be until she has helped teach the student to develop his own evaluation skills to the point where he can trust his own judgement and no longer believe everything he reads.

One would expect similar work to be going on in the classrooms. The authority – virtual sanctity – of the printed word is practically built into the process of learning to read. We *believe* the label on the bottle that warns, 'Not to be taken', or the sign in the cinema that directs us to the exit. The librarian can put before her readers books with diametrically opposing views, and she can provide materials with contrary viewpoints to teachers using textbooks in class, so that they can do the same.

Another possible strategy for demystifying print that involves not only the school but the whole community, is the making of books. The Thomas Coram Research Unit is one agency that developed this idea; an infant school in which I researched was another. In this school, parents were invited to make books for their children and did so in a range of home languages from French to Urdu. In a junior community school it was the children who wrote their own. In all cases these writings (and often illustrations) went to a technician, and were printed and laminated to a respectable and sturdy standard. What happened to them next is particularly significant: they became part of the general library stock in the school. One strategy for indicating the mere mortality and fallibility of authors, and the reality that every author is in some way biased!

Developing Teaching Materials

Where the school is, in a more conventional way, developing its own teaching materials, the librarian has a role in first ascertaining that nothing commercially produced, or available from another school, teachers' centre or another LEA, would do the job equally well. She should continue to be involved in the actual development, so that she can work with the teachers to ensure that a multicultural, anti-racist and anti-sexist approach is taken in formulating the new resource.

Selection of Materials

The area in which the librarian still has most influence is in the selection of stock. While she cannot take sole responsibility for the content of all the materials – which may well number over 10,000 – in the library, she is still the one member of staff with the defined role and professional skills and resources to sift through publications old and new. She would, however, need the support of the teachers, or possibly a small team of them, in evaluating existing materials and choosing new ones, particularly in defined curriculum areas.

The librarian may find it necessary to develop her own evaluation skills, relying for a time, perhaps, on the numerous printed criteria for selection[5] and familiarising herself and the selection committee with some of the rationale as explained by a number of writers: such as Bob Dixon (1977), Sara Zimet (1976) and Marion Glastonbury (1982). But far more effective is for a team in the school – perhaps the working party for equality in education, where there is one – along with the library team, to consider materials and while so doing develop their *own* selection criteria. These criteria could then form part of any anti-racist/anti-sexist policy document of the school.

The argument against using racist books in an unmonitored way in schools, and particularly school libraries, is probably won. Attacks on the almost absurd sexism of reading schemes has filtered upwards to a growing awareness that sexism is also a reality of most story books and information books (Burgess, 1981). There is a growing literature on the subject of bias in books, starting with *Sowing the Dragon's Teeth* by Dorothy Kuya, published by the Liverpool Community Relations Council in 1971. Ten years on, Rampton (DES, 1981a) and the Home Affairs Committee (1981), both recommended that racist materials in schools be replaced, though Bullock (DES, 1975) challenged their use in 1975. Here, I shall content myself with a reference to Frank Whitehead's research for the Schools Council in the 1970s (Whitehead, 1977) one outcome of which was to show that, even though children know where the fiction begins and ends, what they *do* take on unquestioningly is 'the values and attitudes of the author', and it is these values and attitudes that form a 'residue' in the child's mind.

The good school library will have space for students to discuss with the librarian or among themselves, what they have read and what to read next – or, failing space, scheduled times where it can happen in an unforced and informal way. The good school librarian will be well read and up-to-date in her fiction stock and so able to discuss the books. She will create opportunities to draw students' attention to novels and poetry, and should ensure that, whatever the composition of the school, the library includes books that are non-sexist and those which give insights into the views and the experiences of a diversity of racial and cultural groups.

No school librarian can hope to be a constant buffer between the readers and what they read. This has enormous implications for the selection of library resources. While teachers, arguably, can use *any* materials in the classroom, including the overtly racist and sexist, as long as they are sensitive to the messages and can challenge them as they arise – otherwise, they appear to condone them – the librarian has to be more rigorous about what she puts on the open library shelves. And certainly this is especially true for young children, who haven't yet been trained towards a healthy scepticism and a confidence in their own judgement. 'Selection versus censorship' is an ongoing and to some extent spurious debate.[6] It is explored in *Reading into Racism* (Klein, 1985), and is focused on in *Multicultural Teaching* 2.1. (Autumn 1983), both in the editorial, and in articles by David Buckingham and Christine Shawcross. Shawcross, in her article, 'Sense and Censorship', identifies a stance taken by certain school librarians of, 'Who are *we* to tell students what they should read?' and demonstrates that this apparent liberality is in reality a 'cop-out'. Certainly, I have yet to see copies of *Mein Kampf* or *Did Six Million Really Die?* on the open shelves of any school library or, for that matter, volumes on paedophilia or hard pornography. In practical terms, all librarians censor. When they select resources, they have to leave things out. Librarians also regularly 'weed' the shelves – of the tatty, the outdated and the unused; if they remove also the overtly racist and sexist which have not automatically fallen in the weeding process, they are open to further accusations of censorship. Open also to a valid criticism argued by Buckingham, viz. that a school library stock 'cleansed' of all racist materials (should this be possible) would present an extremely distorted view of the world, one that did not in any way square with the reality. There are no simple solutions or rigid rules. Librarians will be guided, as in most matters, by their own principles and the educational objectives of their schools, as they make pragmatic decisions over individual books and learning aids.

Rather than sanitising their collections, librarians can best seek to sensitise their readers. Teachers and librarian can work together in the school to take on the common-sense racism reflected in English publications overall. Strategies to combat it will vary: first, however, bias must be readily recognised. This skill needs, therefore, to be developed by staff, including the librarian, looking together at areas of the curriculum and the textbooks, films and background reading books through which each subject is taught.

But a good school library ranges far beyond the school syllabus and the collection contains its own message. It is still all too easy for the librarian to buy a few 'multiracial' novels, a couple of Chinese cookery books, one or two on steelband and sitar, and see her library as now being 'multicultural'. All she will have done is to parallel the actions of the imaginary teachers evoked by Salman Rushdie (Rushdie, 1982) and Maureen Stone (Stone, 1981) when they describe multicultural education as 'steel band or how to tie a sari'. And the library is a key area in the school from which to beam out the fact that in all areas of activity and belief there is a wide variety of values and norms. No one set of such values and norms is inherently superior; equally, no one – inevitably Anglocentric – accepted set of values and standards, one approved body of knowledge, is inherently superior with everything else deviant and different, at best exotic and quaint.

As well as increasing her sensitivity and skills, as well as consultation with colleagues and community, there are certain *selection procedures* that the librarian can follow in pursuit of building an appropriate stock.

(i)   Books and audio-visual materials should be examined before purchase, whether at bookshops, at special educational or commercial exhibitions, or in the consultative collections set up by an increasing number of education authorities, such as ILEA's Centre for Urban Educational Studies,[7] or by the school library support services found in many areas.

(ii) Publishers' catalogues should be used only for details for ordering, never for selection. Even new titles in a series that has proved its worth cannot be relied upon to be acceptable.

(iii) Reviews may be more reliable, particularly when one has come to trust that reviewer (these days, reviews are signed) or journal, but should be used only with caution.

(iv) Specialised lists of children's books for a multicultural society, and some non-sexist bibliographies are available,[8] but again the librarian should base her final choice on her own assessment of the books and her users.

(v)   Purchasing should not be restricted totally to central supply avenues – although a few authorities are widening these to admit books in community languages and from alternative publishers. Finance should also be available for on-the-spot purchase of books on sale at exhibitions and conferences and at specialist bookshops.

(vi) Guidance should be sought from advisers or parents on the selection, particularly of books in the pupils' home languages, where available. (Whether or not the pupils are literate in their home languages, the recognition by the school that their language, too, has a literature has been seen to mean a good deal to bilingual children and is a salutory point to make to English children, too.)

Consideration may need to be given also to *existing stock*. When routinely weeding shabby, outdated or never-read stock, the librarian can be on the alert also for overtly sexist and racist materials, and will have to make decisions about what to do with them. The same financial pressures which mean we can never buy as many resources as we want and cannot afford to waste a penny on inappropriate purchases, may incline us to preserve resources which appear to have even a little usefulness.

By drawing teachers' attention to biased materials in their subject areas, the librarian can involve the whole school in developing a policy on biased books. This has led in some instances to the school proceeding next to considering anti-sexist and anti-racist policies. With the library stock making a positive contribution to equality in education in the school, librarians should move out into the school and work with the staff towards a unified approach towards issues of sex and class, culture and race.

It must have become evident that school librarians themselves may need to reassess their *function in schools*. For a start, they may gain much from in-service training that focuses on social and educational theory and practice, rather than on administrative, indexing and selection skills in which they have already had good initial training. They should be encouraged and enabled to attend such courses – which means also that structures exist to free them from their libraries – and schools and LEAs should ensure that they have the opportunities to attend courses for teachers on sex equality and multicultural education.

And, finally, school librarians need to identify their professional obligations as differing from those of librarians in the public sector. Librarians are, rightly, in a service role. But being client-bases in a school is rather different from responding to the demands of public borrowers, who are themselves generally only a small proportion of the community, and an unrepresentative one at that. The school librarian is so placed as to serve *all* the school population, and her objectives may be better related to the educational objectives of the school than to a response to individual demands, though she may meet these too.

So, while the school library, when it presents a varied and well-selected stock, may be reflecting the cultural diversity in the school, this should not be its only function. The school population may be monocultural, but the resources should not be. It could be argued that it is in precisely those areas where classmates, teachers and even the shops, signs, food-stalls in the High Street do *not* reflect diversity, that published resources that do so are particularly needed. The school library may be the first agency to make its readers aware that *not* only white people exist, that *more* than the middle class matters, and that it isn't even true that boys will be boys and girls will be good.

NOTES

1 *Specific journals*:
   Interracial Books for Children (eight p.a.), CIBC, 1841 Broadway, New York, NY 10023, USA.
   Multicultural Education Abstracts (quarterly), Carfax Publishing, P.O. Box 25, Abingdon, Oxfordshire, OX14 1RW.
   Multicultural Teaching to Combat Racism in School and Community (three p.a.), Trentham Books, 30 Wenger Road, Trentham, Stoke-on-Trent, ST4 8LE.
   Multicultural Education, Birmingham Education Authority
   and
   Cassoe newsletter, 7 Pickwick Court, London, SE9 4SA.
   Spare Rib, 27 Clerkenwell Close, London, EC1.
   Women in Education, 14 St Brendon's Road, Withington, Manchester 20.
   Women in Libraries, 8 Hill Road, London NW8.
   Women's Studies Quarterly, Pergamon Press, Headington Hill Hall, Oxford, OX3 0BW.

2 A small selection of *novels* can be found in:
   KLEIN, GILLIAN (1982) *Schools Council Resources for Multicultural Education: An Introduction*, Section 5 'Reading for pleasure'. They can be supplemented with Heinemann's African and Caribbean Writers' Series.

3 *Library administration in schools*:
   DYER, C. *et al.* (1970) *School Libraries, Theory and Practice.* London: Clive Bingley.
   GORDON, CECILIA (1977) *Resource Organisation in Primary Schools.* CET/School Library Association.
   SCHOOL LIBRARY ASSOCIATION (1972) *Libraries in secondary schools*, and, for an exposition of educational theory in relation to the school library:
   BESWICK, NORMAN (1977) *Resource-based Learning.* London: Heinemann.

4 DEWEY Decimal Classification: The two editions most used in schools (and considered here) are: *The Abridged Dewey Decimal Classification and Relative Index*, edition 10 (1971) and *Introduction to Dewey Decimal Classification for British Schools* (1961) both published by Forest Press, New York.

5 *Selection Criteria*
   The most comprehensive, prepared by the World Council of Churches, can be found in:
   PREISWERK, ROY (1980) *The Slant of the Pen: Racism in children's books.* WCC.
   Briefer guides include:
   JONES, C. and KLEIN, G. (1980) *Assessing children's books for the multi-ethnic society; practical guidelines.* ILEA.

NATIONAL UNION OF TEACHERS (1981) *In Black and White*. The CRE also distribute a checklist for sexism and racism in children's books.

6 *Selection or Censorship?*
  KLEIN, G. (1985) *Reading into Racism: Bias in Children's Literature and Learning Resources*. London: Routledge and Kegan Paul.
  BUCKINGHAM, DAVID: 'Positive images' and SHAWCROSS, CHRISTINE: 'Sense and censorship', both in the 'Resources' issue of *Multicultural Teaching for Practitioners in School and Community*, **2**, 1, Autumn 1983.

7 Centre for Urban Educational Studies (CUES), Robert Montefiore Building, Underwood Road, London, E1 (telephone 01-377 0040). Includes a consultative collection of appropriate fiction and curriculum materials for schools, and information books, periodicals, video cassettes, etc., for teachers. Visit by appointment with the librarian.

An increasing number of LEAs have multicultural resource centres. Two of the most established in London are Brent and Haringey; beyond are Bedfordshire, Coventry, Birmingham. A full list is available from MERC, Denbigh School, Denbigh Road, Luton, Beds.

In some regions, the School Library Support Services have special collections, e.g. Bradford. Particularly recommended for their thorough and sensitive reviews included in all new books displayed are the central consultative collections for schools provided by the Library Services of Leicester and Nottinghamshire.

8 DIXON, BOB (1982) *Now read on*. London: Pluto Press.
  STONES, ROSEMARY (1982) *Penguin Multiethnic Booklist*.

CUES publishes short selected lists, regularly updated, including: *Non-sexist Books, Books for Children, Books for Under-Fives in our Multicultural Society*.

This chapter was completed in April 1983.

References and Bibliography

AFRO-CARIBBEAN EDUCATIONAL RESOURCE PROJECT (ACER) (1982) *Racism and the Black Child*: Follow-up Groups. Submission to Rampton/Swann Committee.

ALLADINA, S. (1983) 'Languages in Britain – Perceptions and Policies in Education', in *Report* of 1982 Conference organised by National Convention of Black Teachers.

ANWAR, M. (1979) *The Myth of Return: Pakistanis in Britain*. London: Heinemann.

ANWAR, M. (1983) 'Education and the Muslim Community in Britain', *Muslim Education*, 1, 3, 1982, pp. 9–23.

ANYON, J. (1981) 'Social Class and School Knowledge', *Curriculum Enquiry*, 11, pp. 3–42.

BARKER, M. (1981) *The New Racism*. London: Junction Books.

BARTON, L. and WALKER, S. (eds) (1983) *Race, Class and Education*. Beckenham: Croom Helm.

BERKSHIRE LOCAL EDUCATION AUTHORITY (1982) *Education for Equality*. Paper prepared for the Advisory Committee on Multicultural Education, Royal County of Berkshire Education Authority.

BERKSHIRE LOCAL EDUCATION AUTHORITY (1983) *Education for Racial Equality* (Policy Papers 1, 2, 3). Royal County of Berkshire.

BOHM, D. (1980) *Wholeness and the Implicate Order*. London: Routledge and Kegan Paul.

BOURDIEU, P. and PASSERON, J. C. (1977) *Reproduction in Education, Society and Culture*. London: Sage Publications.

BOWLES, S. and GINTIS, L. (1976) *Schooling in Capitalist America: Educational Reform and the Contradictions of Economic Life*. New York: Basic Books.

BRAITHWAITE, L. (1952) 'Social Stratification in Trinidad', *Social and Economic Studies*, 2 (2, 3).

BRAVERMAN, H. (1974) *Labour and Monopoly Capital*. New York: Monthly Review Press.

BREINBERG, P. (1980) 'Who is writing what and for whom?', *West Indian Digest*.

BRENT EDUCATION COMMITTEE (with Brent Teachers' Association, NUT) (1980) *Multicultural Education in Brent Schools*. Brent LEA and Brent NUT.

BRENT EDUCATION COMMITTEE (1982) *Report 44/182*. Brent LEA.

BRENT LOCAL EDUCATION AUTHORITY (1983) *Education for a Multicultural Democracy*, Books 1 and 2. London Borough of Brent Education Committee.

BROADBENT, J. et al. (1983) *Assessment in a Multicultural Society: Community Languages at 16+*. York: Longman for Schools Council.

BURGESS, C. (1981) 'Counteracting Stereotyping in the Primary School', *Dragon's Teeth*, 13, 2.

CAMPAIGN AGAINST RACISM AND FASCISM (CARF)/SOUTHALL RIGHTS (1981) *Southall: The Birth of a Black Community*. London: Southall Rights and Inter-race Relations.

CAPRA, F. (1977) *The Tao of Physics*. New York: Bantam.

CAPRA, F. (1983) *The Turning Point*. New York: Flamingo.

CARRINGTON, BRUCE (1983) 'Sport as a Side-track. An analysis of West Indian Involvement in Extra Curricular Sport', in BARTON, L. and WALKER, S. (eds) *Race, Class and Education*. Beckenham: Croom Helm.

CASHMORE, ERNEST (1979) *Rastaman: The Rastafarian Movement in England*. London: Allen and Unwin.

CASTLES, S. and KOSACK, G. (1973) *Immigrant Workers in the Class Structure in Western Europe*. London: Oxford University Press.

CENTRE FOR CONTEMPORARY CULTURAL STUDIES (1981) *Unpopular Education*. London: Hutchinson.

CENTRE FOR CONTEMPORARY CULTURAL STUDIES (1982) *The Empire Strikes Back: Race and Racism in '70s Britain*. London: Hutchinson.

COLEMAN, J. S., CAMPBELL, E. O., HOBSON, C. J., MCPARTLAND, J., MOOD, A. M., WIENFELD, F. D., and YORK, R. L. (1966) *Equality of Educational Opportunity*. Washington, DC: US Government Printing Office.

COTTLE, T. J. (1978) *Black Testimony: Voices of Britain's West Indians*. London: Wildwood.

DAVIES, B. (1981) *Restructuring Youth Policies in Britain: The State We're In*. National Youth Bureau Occasional Paper.

DAVIS, G. (1981) 'Assumptions underlying current practices in Multicultural Education'. Paper for Research Seminar of Centre for Multicultural Education, University of London Institute of Education.

DEPARTMENT OF EDUCATION AND SCIENCE (1973) *Careers Education in Secondary Schools*. London: HMSO.

DEPARTMENT OF EDUCATION AND SCIENCE (1975) *A Language for Life* (the Bullock Report). London: HMSO.

DEPARTMENT OF EDUCATION AND SCIENCE (1977a) *Circular 14/77.* London: HMSO.

DEPARTMENT OF EDUCATION AND SCIENCE (1977b) *Education in Schools: A Consultative Document.* London: HMSO.

DEPARTMENT OF EDUCATION AND SCIENCE (1978a) *Circular 15/78.* London: HMSO.

DEPARTMENT OF EDUCATION AND SCIENCE (1978b) *Special Educational Needs: Report of the Committee of Enquiry into the Education of Handicapped Children and Young People* (the Warnock Report). London: HMSO.

DEPARTMENT OF EDUCATION AND SCIENCE (1981a) *West Indian Children in Our Schools.* Interim Report of the Committee of Enquiry into the education of children from ethnic minority groups (the Rampton Report). London: HMSO.

DEPARTMENT OF EDUCATION AND SCIENCE (1981b) *The School Curriculum.* London: HMSO.

DEPARTMENT OF EDUCATION AND SCIENCE (1982) *Circular 6/82, The Youth Training Scheme: Implications for the Education Service.* London: HMSO.

DEPARTMENT OF EDUCATION AND SCIENCE (1985) *Education for All* (the Swann Report). London: HMSO.

DEPARTMENT OF EDUCATION AND SCIENCE (jointly with DEPARTMENT OF EMPLOYMENT) (1984) *Training for Jobs.* London: HMSO.

DHEER, RANJIT (1982) 'ILEA and Multiethnic Education', *Shakti,* May.

DHONDY, FARRUKH, BEESE, BARBARA and HASSAN, LEILA (1982) *The Black Explosion in British Schools.* London: Race Today.

DIXON, B. (1977) *Catching Them Young. Vol. 1, Sex, Race and Class in Children's Fiction.* London: Pluto Press.

DONALDSON, M. (1978) *Children's Minds.* Glasgow: Fontana.

EGGLESTON, S. J., DUNN, D. K. and PUREWAL, A. (1981) *In-Service Teacher Education in a Multiracial Society.* Keele: University of Keele.

ELLIS, C. (1980) 'All Work and no Play', *Youth in Society,* April, p. 17.

ENGELS, F. (1844; reprinted 1969) *The Condition of the Working Class in England.* London: Panther.

FALLOWS, L. (1983) *Assessment in a Multicultural Society: English at 16 +.* York: Longman for Schools Council.

FEYERABEND, P. (1974) *Against Method.* London: New Left Books.

FEYERABEND, P. (1982) *Science in a Free Society.* London: New Left Books.

FIGUEROA, J. J. (1971) *Society, Schools and Progress in the West Indies.* Pergamon: Oxford.

FIGUEROA, P. and PERSAUD, G. (1976) *Sociology of Education: A Caribbean Reader.* Oxford: Oxford University Press.

FILE, N. and POWER, C. (1981) *Black Settlers in Britain, 1555-1958.* London: Heinemann.

FONER, N. (1979) *Jamaica Farewell: Jamaican Migrants in London*. London: Routledge and Kegan Paul.

FOOT, P. (1965) *Immigration and Race in British Politics*. Harmondsworth: Penguin Books.

FOSTER, M. (1979) 'Do children have views about stereotypes?', *Dragon's Teeth*.

FREIRE, P. (1972) *Pedagogy of the Oppressed*. Harmondsworth: Penguin Books.

FRIEND, A. and METCALF, A. (1981) *Slump City*. London: Pluto Press.

FULLER, M. (1983) 'Qualified Criticism, Critical Qualifications', in BARTON, L. and WALKER, S. (eds) *Race, Class and Education*. Beckenham: Croom Helm.

FURTHER EDUCATION UNIT (1981) *Vocational Preparation*. London: HMSO.

GEISS, EMANUEL (1974) *The Pan-African Movement* (trans. Ann Keep). London: Methuen.

GILES, R. (1977) *The West Indian Experience in British Schools: Multiracial Education and Social Disadvantage in London*. London: Heinemann.

GIROUX, H. A. (1983) 'Theories of Reproduction and Resistance in the New Sociology of Education: A Critical Analysis', *Harvard Educational Review*, 53, 3, pp. 257–93.

GLASTONBURY, M. (1982) 'What books tell girls', *English Magazine*, 9.

GLAZER, N. and MOYNIHAM, D. P. (1963) *Beyond the Melting Pot*. Cambridge, MA: Harvard University Press.

GOULD, S. J. (1984) *The Mismeasure of Man*. Harmondsworth: Penguin Books.

GOULDNER, A. M. (1971) *The Coming Crisis in Western Sociology*. New York: Avon Books.

GOVERNMENT EXPENDITURE PLANS (1981) *1981–2, 1983–4*. London: HMSO.

GRACE, G. (1980) 'Facing the Contradictions', *Teaching London Kids*, 15. London: TLK Collective.

GREEN, A. (1982) *Under New Masters*. Unpublished paper.

Guardian, The (1983), 12 September.

GUNDARA, J. S. (1981) *Multicultural Education: Some Contemporary Problems and Critiques*. Centre for Multicultural Education, University of London Institute of Education.

HALL, S. (1978) 'Racism and Reaction', in *Five Views of Multiracial Britain*. London: Commission for Racial Equality.

HALL, S. (1979) 'Teaching Race', *Multicultural Education*, 9, 1; also in JAMES, A. and JEFFCOATE, R. (1981) *The School in the Multicultural Society*. London: Harper and Row.

HALSEY, A. H. *et al.* (1980) *Origins and Destinations: Family Class and Education in Modern Britain*. Oxford: Clarendon Press.

HARGREAVES, A. (1982) 'Resistance and Relative Autonomy Theories: Problems of Distortion and Incoherence in Recent Marxist

Analyses of Education', *The British Journal of Sociology of Education*, 3, 2, pp. 107–26.

HICKS, D. (1981) *Images of the World: An Introduction to Bias in Teaching Materials*. Centre for Multicultural Education, University of London Institute of Education.

HILL, DAVID (1970) 'The Attitudes of West Indian and English Adolescents in Britain', *New Community*, XI, 3, January 1970.

HOGBEN, L. (1938 et seq.) *Science for the Citizen*. London: Allen and Unwin.

HOGBEN, L. (1967) *Mathematics for the Million*. London: Pan.

HOME AFFAIRS COMMITTEE (1981) *Racial Disadvantage. Vol. 1, Report with minutes of proceedings*. House of Commons Paper 424-I, Session 80/81. London: HMSO.

HOME OFFICE (1981) *The Brixton Disorders, 10–12 April 1981* (the Scarman Report). London: HMSO.

HUSBAND, C. (ed.) (1975) *White Media and Black Britain*. London: Arrow Books.

ILLICH, I. (1976) *Limits to Medicine: Medical Nemesis*. New York: Marion Boyars.

INNER LONDON EDUCATION AUTHORITY (1977) *Multiethnic Education*. Joint Report of the Schools Sub-committee and the Further and Higher Education Sub-committee on 8 November 1977. (A progress report was published in June 1979.)

INNER LONDON EDUCATION AUTHORITY (1983a, b, c, d, e, f) *Race, Sex and Class* (six booklets): 1 *Achievement in School*; 2 *Multiethnic Education in Schools*; 3 *A Policy for Equality: Race*; 4 *Antiracist Statement and Guidelines*; 5 *Multiethnic Education in Further, Higher and Community Education*; 6 *A policy for Equality: Sex*. London: ILEA.

JACKSON, E. (1983) *The Times*, 15 July.

JAMDAIGNI, L., PHILIPS-BELL, M. and WARD, J. (1982) *Talking Chalk: Black Pupils, Parents and Teachers Speak about Education*. Birmingham: All Faiths for One Race (AFFOR).

JAMES, A. (1979) 'The Multicultural Curriculum', *New Approaches in Multicultural Education*, 8, 1.

JENCKS, C., SMITH, M., ACKLAND, H., BANE, M. J., COHEN, G., GINTIS, N., HEYNS, D. and MICHELSON, S. (1972) *Inequality: A Reassessment of the Effect of Family and Schooling in America*. New York: Basic Books.

JENKINS, D. and SHIPMAN, M. (1976) *Curriculum: An Introduction*. London: Open Books.

JONES, C. and KIMBERLEY, K. (1982) 'Educational Responses to Racism', in TIERNEY, J. (ed.) *Race, Migration and Schooling*. London: Holt Education.

KAPO, R. (1981) *A Savage Culture: Racism – A Black British View*. London: Quarto.

KLEIN, G. (1985) *Reading into Racism: Bias in Children's Literature and Learning Resources*. London: Routledge and Kegan Paul.

KLEIN, G. (1985) 'School Libraries for Multicultural Awareness', *Educational Libraries Bulletin*, Supp. 23, University of London Institute of Education and Trentham Books.

KUHN, T. (1962) *The Structure of Scientific Revolutions*. Chicago, IL: University of Chicago Press.

KUYA, D. (1971) *Sowing the Dragon's Teeth*. Liverpool: Liverpool CRC.

LAKATOS, I. and MUSGRAVE, A. (eds) (1970) *Criticism and the Growth of Knowledge*. Cambridge: Cambridge University Press.

LASH, SUSANNAH (1983) 'YTS – Some Fundamental Flaws', *NATFHE Journal*, October.

LAWTON, D. (1980) *The Politics of the School Curriculum*. London: Routledge and Kegan Paul.

LEA, J. and YOUNG, J. (1982) 'A Missed Opportunity', *New Socialist*,

LEE, J. and WRENCH, G. (1981) 'A Clash of Cultures: Youth, Race and Conflict', *Youth in Society*, November.

LÉVI-STRAUSS, C. (1968) *The Savage Mind*. London: Weidenfeld and Nicholson.

LITTLE, A. and WILLEY, R. (1981) *Multiethnic Education: The Way Forward*. Pamphlet 18. London: Schools Council.

LONDON WEEKEND TELEVISION (1982) 'Twentieth Century Box', 11 July.

MCPHERSON, G. H. (1972) *Small Town Teacher*. Cambridge, MA: Harvard University Press.

MANPOWER SERVICES COMMISSION (1981a) *Manpower Review*. London: MSC.

MANPOWER SERVICES COMMISSION (1981b) *A New Training Initiative*. London: MSC.

MANPOWER SERVICES COMMISSION (1982) *London Employment and Review*. London: MSC.

MARTIN, TONY (1976) *Race First*. Westport, CT: Greenwood Press.

MILLER, J. (1983) *Many Voices*. London: Routledge and Kegan Paul.

MILNER, D. (1975) *Children and Race*. Harmondsworth: Penguin Books.

MILNER, D. (1983) *Children and Race: Ten Years On*. London: Ward Lock.

MULLARD, C. (1980) *Racism in Society and Schools: History, policy and practice*. Centre for Multicultural Education, University of London Institute of Education.

MULLARD, C. (1983) 'The Racial Code: Its Features, Rules and Changes', in BARTON, L. and WALKER, S. (eds) *Race, Class and Education*. Beckenham: Croom Helm.

NAGRA, J. S. (1981–2) 'Asian Supplementary School: A case study of Coventry', *New Community*, IX, 3, 1981/2, pp. 431–6.

NATIONAL UNION OF TEACHERS (1982) *Education for a Multicultural Society: Evidence to the Swann Committee of Inquiry submitted by the National Union of Teachers*. London: NUT.

NEEDHAM, J. (1979) *The Grand Titration*. London: Allen and Unwin.

NEEDHAM, J. (1980) *Shorter Science Civilisation in China – Vol. 1.* Cambridge: Cambridge University Press.

PARMAR, P. (1982) 'Gender, Race and Class: Asian Women in Resistance', in CENTRE FOR CONTEMPORARY CULTURAL STUDIES (1982) *The Empire Strikes Back.* London: Hutchinson.

PARSONS, T. (1959) 'The School Class as a Social System: Some of its Functions in American Society', *Harvard Educational Review*, 29, pp. 297–318.

PEDERSEN, E. and ETHERIDGE, K. (1970) 'Conformist and Deviant Behaviour in High School: The Merton Typology Adapted to an Educational Context', *Canadian Review of Sociology and Anthropology*, 7, 1, pp. 70–81.

PEDERSEN, E. and PEDERSEN, M. (1982) *Teaching by Rules: The Development of a Destructive Style in an Inner-city Grade One.* Montreal: McGill University (Xerox).

PEDERSEN, H. and FAUCHER, T. A. with EATON, W. W. (1978) 'A New Perspective on the Effects of First-grade Teachers on Children's Subsequent Adult Status', *Harvard Educational Review*, 48, 1, pp. 1–31.

PINES, J. (undated) *Looking at Images.* London: British Film Institute.

POPPER, K. (1969) *Conjectures and Refutations.* London: Routledge and Kegan Paul.

RICHARDSON, R. (1982) 'Culture and Justice: Key Concepts in World Studies and Multicultural Education', in HICKS, D. and TOWNLEY, C. (eds) *Teaching World Studies.* London: Longman.

RIST, R. C. (1970) 'Student Social Class and Teacher Expectations: The Self-fulfilling Prophecy in Ghetto Education', *Harvard Educational Review*, 40, pp. 411–51.

ROBERTS, K. (1984) *Pavane.* Harmondsworth: Penguin.

ROSE, S., LEWONTIN, R. C. and KAMIN, L. J. (1984) *Not in our Genes.* Harmondsworth: Penguin Books.

RUSHDIE, S. (1982) 'The New Empire in Britain', *New Society*, 9 December.

RUTTER, M., MAUGHAN, B., MORTIMORE, P. and OUSTON, J. with SMITH, A. (1979) *Fifteen Thousand Hours: Secondary Schools and their Effects on Children.* Shepton Mallet: Open Books Publishing Ltd.

SCHOOLS COUNCIL REPORT (1972) *Career Education.* London: Schools Council.

SELECT COMMITTEE ON EDUCATION, SCIENCE AND THE ARTS (1982) *The Secondary School Curriculum and Examinations: Second Report.* London: HMSO.

SEWELL, W. H. (1980) 'Sex, Schooling and Occupational Status', *American Journal of Sociology*, 86, pp. 551–83.

SHARP, R. and GREEN, A. (1975) *Education and Social Control: A Study in Progressive Primary Education.* London: Routledge and Kegan Paul.

SMITH, D. (1976) *Racial Discrimination in Britain.* Harmondsworth: Penguin Books.

STONE, M. (1981) *The Education of the Black Child in Britain: The Myth of Multiracial Education.* London: Fontana.

STREET-PORTER, R. (1978) *Race, Children and Cities* (Block 5 of Course E361, Education and the Urban Environment). Milton Keynes: Open University Press.

TAYLOR, M. J. (1981) *Caught Between: A Review of Research into the Education of Pupils of West Indian Origin.* Windsor: NFER-Nelson.

THOMAS, J. J. (1889; reprinted 1969) *Froudacity: West Indian Fables Explained.* London: New Beacon.

TIERNEY, J. (ed.) (1982) *Race, Migration and Schooling.* London: Holt Education.

Times Educational Supplement, The (1983) 15 July; 12 August.

Times Educational Supplement, The (1985) 15 March.

TOMLINSON, S. (1983) *Ethnic Minorities in British Schools: A Review of the Literature, 1960–1982.* London: Heinemann.

TOWNSEND, E. and BRITTAN, E. (1972) *Organisation in Multiracial Schools.* Slough: NFER.

TOWNSEND, H. E. R. (1971) *Immigrant Pupils in England, the LEA Response.* Windsor: NFER.

TWITCHIN, J. and DEMUTH, C. (1981) *Multicultural Education.* London: BBC.

UNESCO (1983) *Racism, Science and Pseudo-Science: Proceedings of the Symposium to examine pseudo-scientific theories invoked to justify racism and racial discrimination, Athens, 1981.* Paris: UNESCO.

VAN DEN BERGHE, P. (1967) *Race and Racism.* New York: John Wiley.

WALKER, M. (1977) *The National Front.* London: Fontana.

WALVIN, J. (1971) *The Black Presence.* London: Orbach and Chambers.

WALVIN, J. (1973) *Black and White: The Negro in British Society, 1555–1945.* London: Allen Lane.

WATTS, S. (1983) 'Science Education for a Multicultural Society', *Multicultural Teaching,* 1, 3.

WHITEHEAD, FRANK (1977) Children and Books. London: Macmillan.

WILLEY, R. (1982a) 'National Study of Great Britain', in GUNDARA, J., JONES, C. and KIMBERLEY, K. *The Marginalisation and Pauperisation of the Second Generation of Migrants in France, the Federal Republic of Germany and Great Britain relating to the Education of the Children of Migrants.* EEC contract 820002.

WILLEY, R. (1982b) *Teaching in Multicultural Britain.* York: Longman for School Council.

WILLIAMS, E. (1951; n.e. 1968) *Education in the British West Indies.* New York: University Press.

WILLIAMS, I. W. (1984) 'Chemistry', in CRAFT, A. and BARDELL, G. (eds) *Curriculum Opportunities in a Multicultural Society.* London: Harper and Row.

WILSON, A. (1978) *Finding a Voice: Asian Women in Britain.* London: Virago.

WOOD, A. (1984) *Assessment in a Multicultural Society: Religious Studies at 16 +*. York: Longman for Schools Council.

WRAY-JAMIESON, MONIKA *et al.* (1980) *Unified Vocational Preparation*. Windsor: NFER.

ZIMET, S. G. (1976) *Print and Prejudice*. London: Hodder and Stoughton.

Index

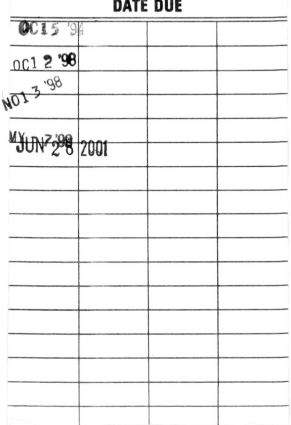